Library of Congress Card Catalog Number: 74-78056

ISBN: 0-87108-083-4

1 2 3 4 5 6 7 8 9

FIRST EDITION

TABLE OF CONTENTS

for Caroline

PREFACE

This book is an introduction to the most prominent animals and plants of the Enchanted Mesa. The kinds of birds and mammals are relatively few, and are well illustrated in the standard field guides that cover larger areas, hence are dealt with here only by text. At the other extreme, the thousands of species of insects that inhabit the mesa live in an obscurity that has only here and there been penetrated by the specialist, and again, only a brief text is devoted to them. It is the trees, shrubs and wildflowers that are most easily seen, and contribute most to the living landscape. We have, accordingly, devoted most of the space available in this booklet to drawings of these. The drawings are presented in the belief that the beginning observer of the mesa wildflowers and other plants can recognize the common species from illustrations that give the general appearance of the plant. For this reason the technical characteristics needed to identify the much larger number of kinds of plants dealt with in manuals completely covering large geographic areas are, in the main, ignored in this introduction to the natural history of the Enchanted Mesa.

Two technical manuals which give identification keys for the entire flora of larger areas that include the mesa are William A. Weber's *Rocky Mountain Flora,* which deals with the Colorado Front Range and the adjacent plains, and H. D. Harrington's *Manual of the Plants of Colorado,* which covers the entire state.

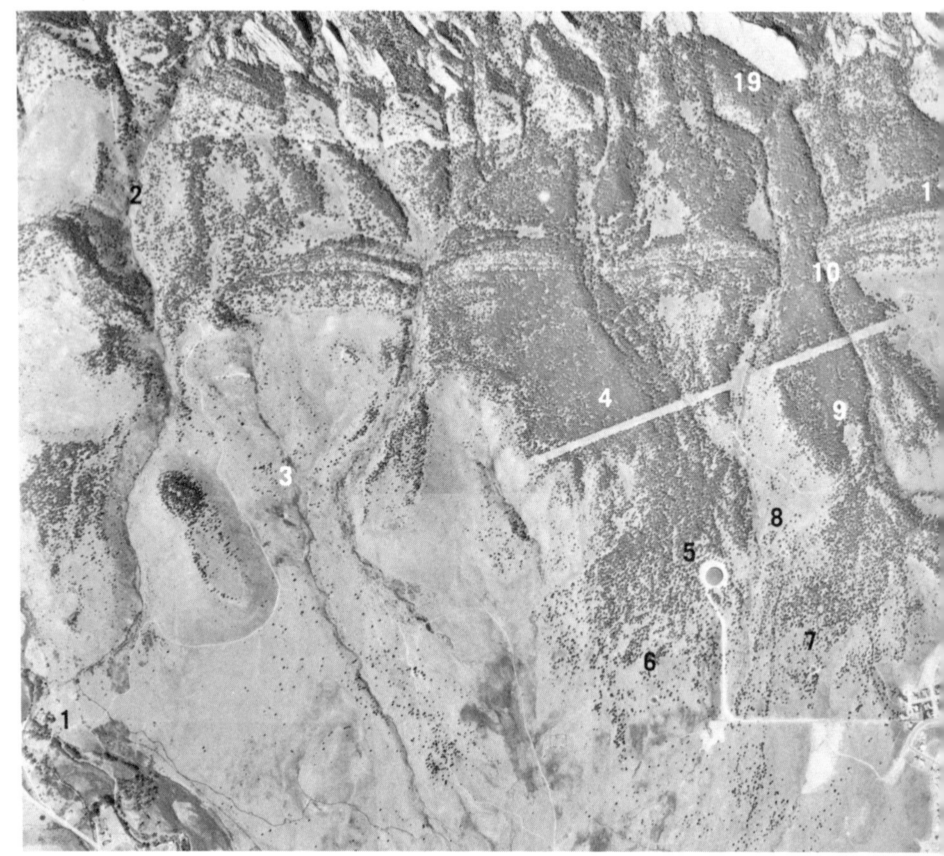

1. Dunn House
2. Shadow canyon
3. Hillside pond
4. Clearing for transmission line
5. City water tank
6. Pollywog pond
7. Abbey pond
8. Salamander pond
9. Shanahan pond
10. Fern canyon

*This aerial photo, taken in 1971, was furnished
by the U. S. Geological Survey*

11. Microwave tower
12. Bear canyon
13. NCAR
14. NCAR water tank
15. Skunk canyon
16. Electric power substation
17. City reservoir
18. Bluebell picnic area
19. The Slab (a "Flatiron", Fountain formation)

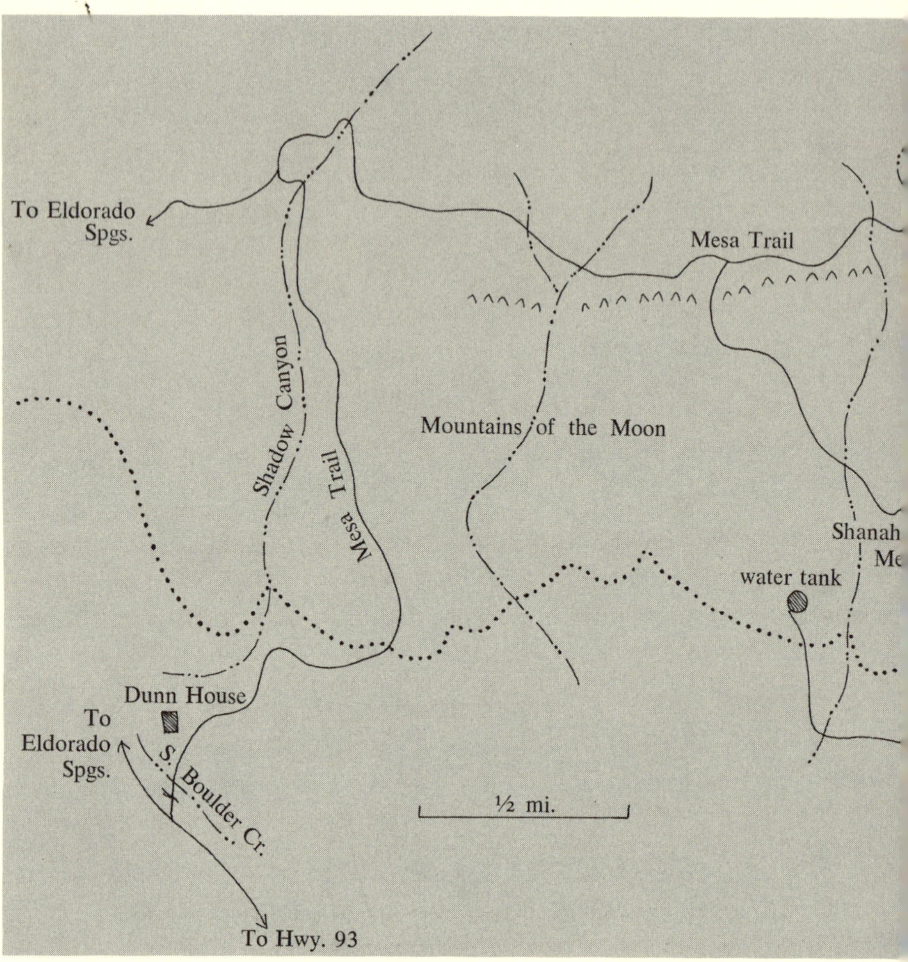

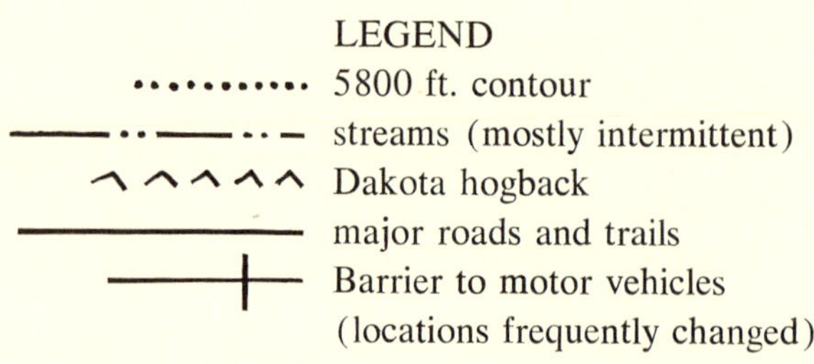

To Eldorado
Spgs.
Mesa Trail
Shadow Canyon
Mesa Trail
Mountains of the Moon
Shanah
Me
water tank
Dunn House
To
Eldorado
Spgs.
S. Boulder Cr.
To Hwy. 93
½ mi.
LEGEND
5800 ft. contour
streams (mostly intermittent)
Dakota hogback
major roads and trails
Barrier to motor vehicles
(locations frequently changed)

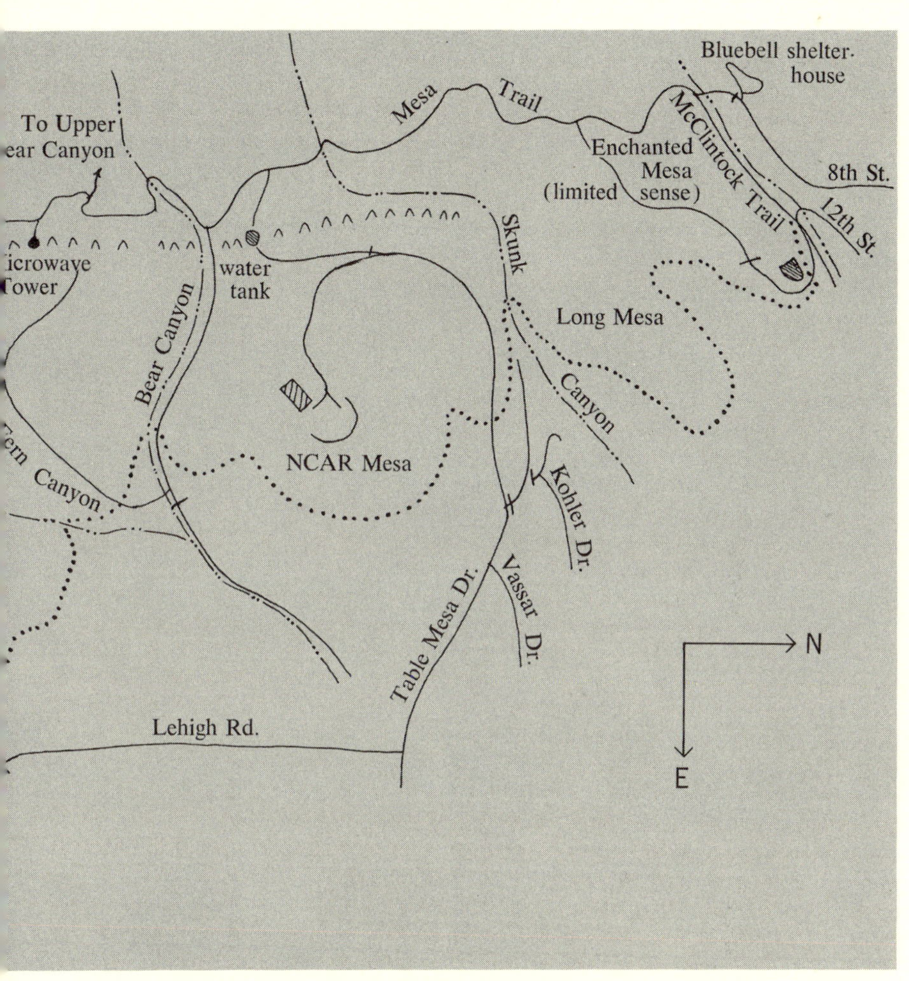

The so-called Mesa Trail lies, for most of its length, just
west of the mesa country, often in a valley west of the Dakota
hogback. From the trail, and from such access areas or points as
the City reservoir (that lies on the southerly continuation of 12th
Street), the west end of Kohler Drive, the Bear Canyon Road,
the south end of Lehigh Road, and the parking area near Dunn
House, which is a mile east of Eldorado Springs, there originates
a maze of small trails and abandoned wagon and motor vehicle
tracks that cover the mesas. Most of these are not shown on this
map. Except for parts of the steep ridge of the Dakota hogback,
which marks the west edge of most of the mesa country, the
Enchanted Mesa is easily passable with or without trails.

Often the 5800 foot contour lies near the foot of the mesa,
the 6000 foot line near the eastern edge of the mesa top.

THE ENCHANTED MESA

Two mountain massifs lie immediately behind Boulder, just west and southwest of the city. These can in a general way be called Green Mountain and Bear Peak, since those are the peaks that from Boulder appear to dominate each of the mountain clusters. So abrupt is the rise of these mountains from the plain that the southwest edge of Boulder, at an altitude of about 5,600 feet, is only a little more than 2 miles away, by straight line on the map, from the summit of Bear Peak, at 8,461 feet. Their looming height makes for winter sunsets in Boulder that occur not much later than 3 o'clock in the afternoon. The east face of these two mountain groups bristles with crags, some of them huge tilted slabs called Flatirons. These cliffs are the third most frequented rock climbing area in the United States.

Fitted up against the base of Green Mountain and Bear Peak like the toes of a cat's paw are several tablelands or mesas, which extend east for a half-mile to a mile, more or less separated from each other by canyons. They are not level, but slope to the east at an angle of 3 or 4 degrees. The mesas, which are only a few hundred feet high, are capped with pine forests, that toward the eastern rims gradually thin out and give way to grassland. Old photos show that during the past century the forest has gradually spread eastward at the expense of the grassland.

Some years ago, it was decided to build a luxury hotel on the northernmost mesa, overlooking the city in such a way as to afford a splendid view for the inhabitants of the hotel, and an inferior view to those below and apart. Either the real estate promoters, perhaps, or the group of activists who became their opponents changed the name of the mesa (the older maps had called it Horse Mesa) to Enchanted Mesa. With a heroic propaganda campaign, the activists persuaded the citizens of Boulder to buy the mesa to add to the park system of the city, which already included Green Mountain and Bear Peak.

The process of thwarting the real estate developers spread south by contagion nearly four miles, all the way to Shadow Canyon and South Boulder Creek, near the settlement of Eldorado Springs. Sometimes all the mesas (often they are not well separated at the western ends, anyway) are referred to collectively as "The Mesa". Here I have decided to use the term Enchanted Mesa for the whole system of tablelands and canyons, nearly all in city parkland, lying between Bluebell Canyon and South Boulder Creek, although often referring to some, such as NCAR Mesa or Shanahan Mesa by individual names.

Somewhere I have seen an old map on which the southern group of mesas were called the "Mountains of the Moon." In Edgar Allen Poe's "Eldorado", a "gallant knight" asks a fellow pilgrim the way:

"Where can it be—
This land of Eldorado?"

"Over the Mountains
Of the Moon,
Down the Valley of the Shadow,
Ride, boldly ride,"
The shade replied,—
If you seek for Eldorado!"

GEOLOGY

Just how the mesas came into existence is something of a mystery; the old and widely accepted theory that they are stream terraces is probably wrong. Most likely they are remnants of "bajadas", the gently sloping bases of mountains in the arid southwest that are produced by the sheet floods from torrential rains that move rocks and gravel down entire mountainsides, rather than only in the confines of stream beds. This is characteristic of arid ranges where there is little vegetation to check erosion. Probably the main outlines of The Mesa took shape in the Pleistocene epoch, a time of dramatic climatic changes, and are therefore relatively young, geologically speaking, perhaps no more than a million years old. During this time, the "bajada" has been carved by streamlets into the modern complex topography of the Enchanted Mesa.

The top layer of the mesas is an unconsolidated mass of debris from Green Mountain and Bear Peak that is 20 to 30 feet thick. This layer contains boulders that in some places are thickly strewn over the surface of the ground. Some are immense—20 or 30 feet in diameter. They are often sculptured by weathering in picturesque fashion, even to having a bird-bath pool on top. Many are covercd with patches of lichens, which are primitive plants composed of a compatible mixture of algae and fungi; such rocks are known in the building trade and to the considerable number of amateur rock robbers as "moss rocks".

Most of the boulders on the mesas are from the Fountain formation, which makes up the Flatirons. A minority are from the Dakota formation which, especially near Bear Canyon, forms the first hogback of the foothills, standing some distance out from the Flatirons. Some also are of the hard, pink or cream-colored Lyons sandstone, into which an abandoned quarry that defaces the city parkland has been dug. Farther north in the foothills the Lyons formation is much thicker, and better suited for quarrying operations. Many of the University of Colorado buildings are faced with Lyons sandstone.

Under the veneer of Pleistocene debris, the bed rock of the mesas is soft limestones and shales of the Benton, Niobrara, and

Pierre formations. These are, like the Flatirons and Dakota hogback, steeply tilted, a tilt that expresses the uplift that produced the Rocky Mountains. Some of the mesa canyons, such as Bear Canyon, have exposed the otherwise hidden limestones and shales. While the Dakota, Lyons, and Fountain formations are almost barren of fossils, the Benton and Niobrara are rich in the remains of animals that lived in a sea that, near the end of the Age of Reptiles, covered the mid-continent from the Arctic Ocean to the Gulf of Mexico. The Niobrara has one or more continuous layers, a half-inch or so thick, of small oyster shells, and scattered shells of other larger kinds of mollusks. There are small clams and fish scales in the black shales of the Benton. The very thick Pierre shales are rather barren, except for some narrow bands of sandstones rich in fossils. In seams and cracks in the Niobrara limestone, especially on the western edge of NCAR Mesa, are plates of the mineral calcite, sometimes forming crude crystals.

In the valley on the west side of the Dakota ridge is the Morrison formation, famous elsewhere for its bones of huge dinosaurs. Here it is usually covered by vegetation, but on the north side of Bear Canyon it is exposed as patches of green, purple, and red clays. An hour-long search here yielded a half-dozen small fragments of disintegrated reptile bone.

VEGETATION

In this introduction to the natural history of the Enchanted Mesa, we will emphasize the plant cover which, in comparison with the animals, dominates the scenery, and is more easily accessible to the observer. The vegetation provides the food base for the animal inhabitants of the mesa, the most abundant of which are the insects and small rodents that feed on the plants. These small animals are generally concealed from casual view, but themselves become the food of predatory animals, especially the birds, most of which feed their young, and sometimes themselves, on the teeming insect population of the mesa.

The vegetation cover is a sensitive indicator of the climatic regime and of the year-to-year variations in climate. The climate of the Boulder area is generally one of wet spring weather and dry summers and winters, but it varies much from year to year. This may greatly alter the smaller, non-woody plants, which one year might be lush giants of their kind, the next dry and dusty dwarfs. With a precipitation of about 18 inches annually, the climate is semi-arid. The forest of hardwoods grown in Boulder is, like the lawns, supported by irrigation. The most dangerous aspects of the climate for the imported trees are the occasional late or early snows and cold spells, that break down leafy branches with the weight of snow, or freeze inner bark tissues not yet prepared for winter or too early supplied with spring sap. Hardly ever are appreciable numbers of the native trees killed in this way.

High above the summits of the mountains is a layer of powerful west winds which, however, in the winter may dip down to the mountaintops, where they blow with hurricane force. One would think that the mesas, sheltered under the lee of high and steep mountains, would escape these winds, but the opposite is true. Striking the tops of Green Mountain and Bear Peak, the wind is deflected downward, tumbling and swirling in the manner of a rough waterfall, so that there may be local gusts with velocities as high as 140 or 150 miles an hour, considerably greater than that of the upper wind stream. These winds damage even the native pine forests of the mesa. The ground may be strewn with branches, the top halves of good-sized trees, and even entire corpses of the oldest giants after one of these wild storms.

TREES

The forest on the mesa tops is a pure stand of Ponderosa pine (or, as it used to be called, Yellow pine), although there are scattered Red cedars and, especially on the higher parts of the mesas, some Douglas firs. In the canyons is a rich tangle of a variety of trees and shrubs, providing an entirely different habitat from that on the mesa tops.

Red cedar; Juniper (*Juniperus virginiana*). A small evergreen tree with silvery green, scale-like leaves. Not common, but the handsome pyramidal form attracts attention. A small grove of cedars is to be found on the Niobrara shale outcrop just southwest of the NCAR complex. The frosty blue berries are a welcome find for overwintering robins.

Douglas fir (*Pseudotsuga menziesii*). At lower elevations, say below 9,000 feet, this evergreen tree is usually restricted to north slopes, but in the dense forests of the western end of the mesas, it occurs on the mesa tops as low as 6,000 feet. The needles are single and soft, the cones small and papery.

Ponderosa pine; Yellow pine (*Pinus ponderosa*). P. 7. By far the most common tree of the mesa forest. North of Colorado Springs, this is usually (the chief exception is a localized forest of Pinyon pines north of Fort Collins) the first species of pine encountered as one goes into the mountains. The long needles are in bundles of two or three. Seeds from its large, heavy-scaled cones are the mainstay of the economy of the Tuft-eared squirrels that live on the mesa. In some places the pines grow close together as a dense stand of small, starved trees, slender as Lodgepole pines. Here the smallest trees are dead or dying, and a deadly competition for light and soil moisture continues as the few victors slowly gain in height. The mature pines of the mesa forest have the crowns open, without a leader.

Boxelder (*Acer negundo*). P. 7. This untidy-looking maple is common along the bottoms of the canyons. In some years the trees are loaded with incredible numbers of the typical two-winged maple fruits. When these ripen, they split into two single-bladed propellers that can carry the heavy seed a good distance in a strong breeze.

Ponderosa
Boxelder

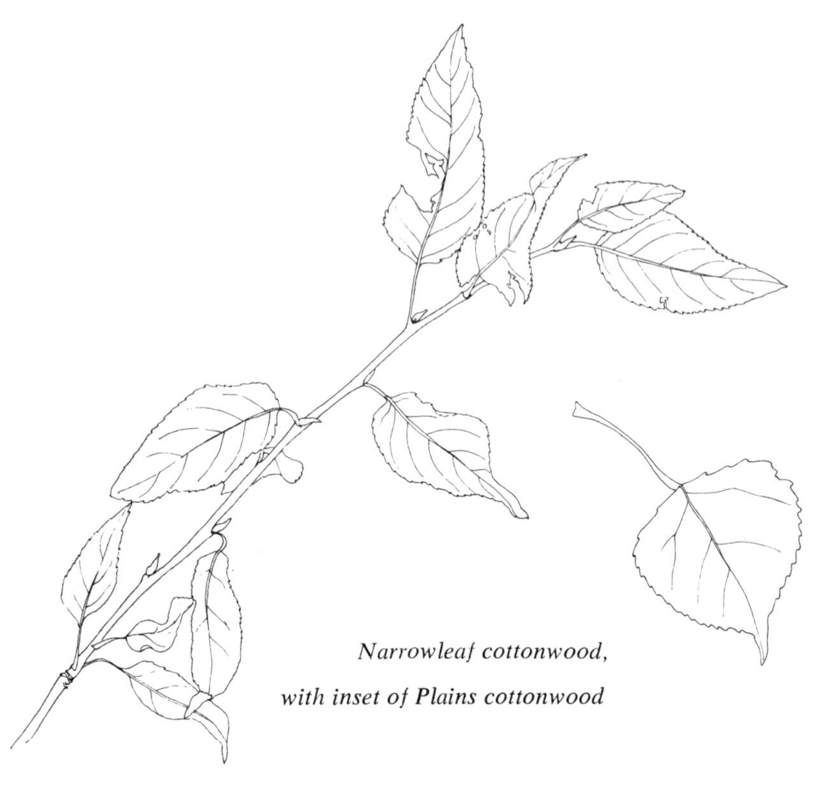

Cottonwoods (*Populus*). P. 8. The most common of the cotton-wood trees in the canyons of the mesa and the higher mountains is the relatively small Narrowleaf cottonwood (*P. angustifolia*), whose slender, willow-like leaves are several times longer than wide (cottonwoods can be distinguished from willows by the fact that the twigs of the latter do not have terminal buds).

A short distance out on the plains, along the stream valleys, is the huge Plains cottonwood (*P. sargentii*) whose broad leaves tremble and shimmer in the sunlight, because of the flattened leaf-stalk (as in the Aspen).

In the lower reaches of the mesa canyons are large cotton-woods with broad leaves that do not have flattened leaf-stalks. These are believed to be hybrids between the Plains and Narrow-leaf cottonwoods, and have in the past been called the Smooth-barked cottonwood. In the upper mesa canyons are occasional Aspens (*Populus tremuloides*), which become abundant at higher altitudes. They can be identified by the white, smooth bark and the broad, finely saw-edged leaves with flat leaf-stalks.

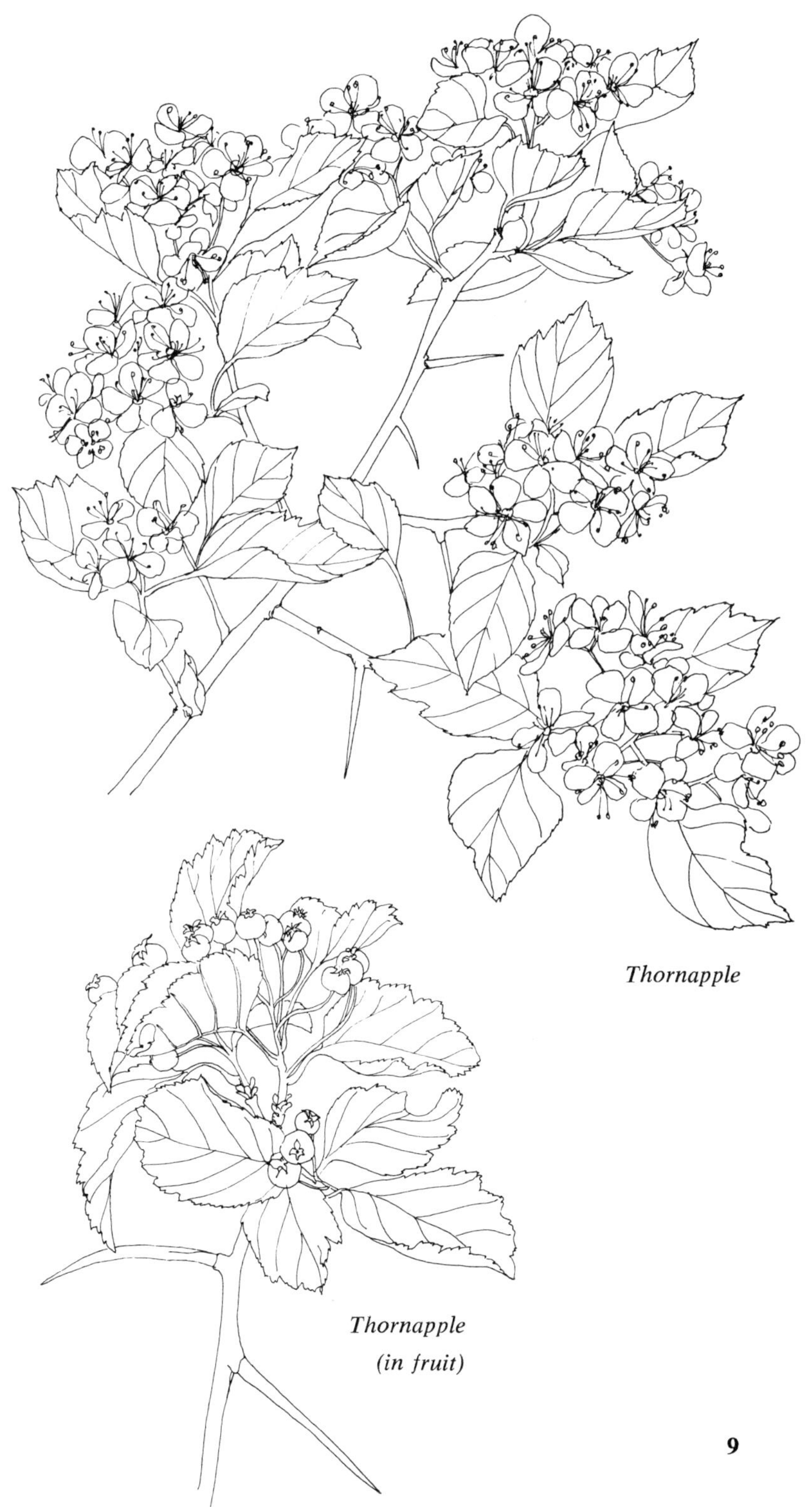

Thornapple

Thornapple
(in fruit)

Wild plum

Thornapple, Hawthorn (*Crataegus*). P. 9. One of the commonest small trees in the mesa valleys, forming impenetrable thorny thickets, the home of towhees, chats, and other birds with unfindable nests. The abundant white flowers are not fragrant, but attract several species of wild bees; the fruits are bright red. Apparently 2 species, which hybridize.

Wild Plum (*Prunus americana*). P. 10. A small, thorny tree that in early spring is covered with sheets of small white flowers, with petals that quickly brown and fall away. The perfume is unique—a mixture of the smell of fresh tortillas and a sweet flowery odor. The flesh of the frosty-purple fruit is delicious, although the skin is sour. Most years the fruits are too few and insect-ridden to be of much interest to the hiker.

SHRUBS

If in doubt whether a large, woody plant is a shrub or tree, look under both headings in this book. At the smaller end of the size spectrum, the shrubs grade well into what the botanists call "herbaceous" plants. Oregon grape, for example, is a shrub only a few inches high. The distinction lies in the woody stems and the above-ground winter resistant buds of the shrubby plants.

Ground Juniper (*Juniperus communis*). A low, dense, flattened bush with short, awl-shaped, needle-sharp leaves, frosty blue berries, and a cedary fragrance.

Hazelnut (*Corylus cornuta*). P. 12. This is one of the shrubs that crowd the cool, moist streamside habitat found in the deeper mesa canyons. This habitat, with hawthornes, maples, hazel, grape and ninebark reminds one of the undergrowth of the eastern forests.

F. P. Daniels, a professor of Romance languages at the University of Missouri, who made a pioneer survey of the plants of the Boulder area in the summer of 1906, wrote of the mesa canyons, "It is true that a closer examination reveals the fact that many of these plants belong to species which are strictly western, yet the fact remains that there is little in the vegetation that impresses as strange, one who is familiar only with the eastern flora, while all about him in plain, mesa and foothill are utterly unfamiliar types of vegetation."

The hazelnut is the same species as the eastern hazelnut and seems to be a left-over from the times when the climate was much different in the Rocky Mountain area. Hazelnuts of the Front Range area are now an isolated colony, being, so far as is known, absent in Wyoming and with their nearest neighbors far to the north in the Black Hills region.

The nuts of this abundant shrub must be extremely popular with the wild animals, since they are rarely found. The structures that contain them come in pairs; the drawing shows only one, the other having been broken off.

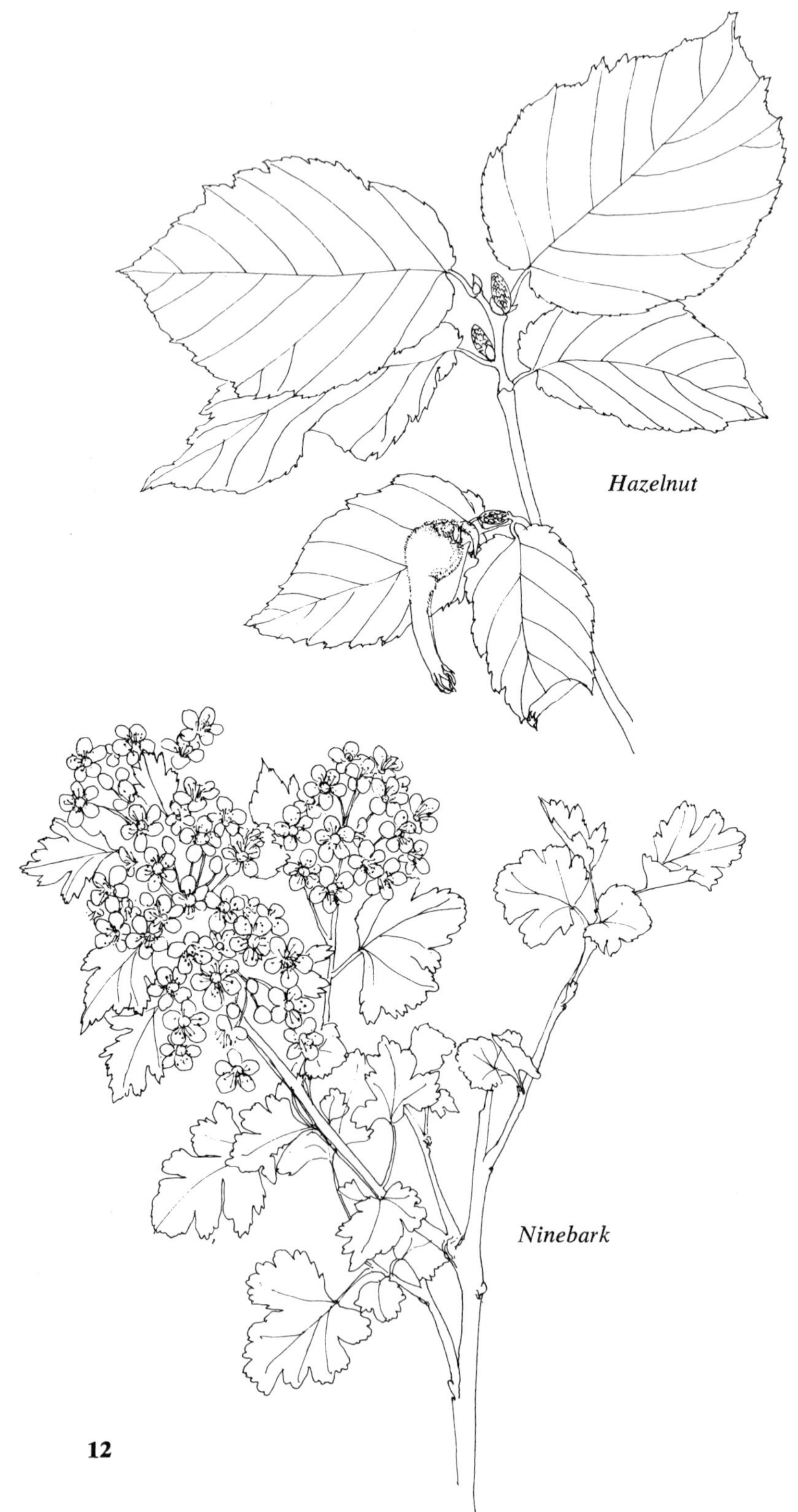

Hazelnut
Ninebark

Sandbar willow

Willows (*Salix*). P. 13. The most common willow along the lower streamlets of the mesa canyons is the Sandbar willow (*S. exigua*), with very narrow leaves and small catkins. At the base of the foothills are other stream-side willows ("pussy willows") with large catkins that appear in early spring, attracting swarms of wild bees.

Wild rose (*Rosa*). P. 15. The wild roses of the mesa vary in size from small plants a few inches in height to bushes several feet high. The species are difficult to identify, perhaps in part because of hybridization.

Ninebark (*Physocarpus monogynus*). P. 12. A white-flowered bush that resembles the garden *Spirea*. The bark peels off in a large number of thin layers.

Mountain mahogany (*Cercocarpus montanus*). P. 16. A relative of the rose, but with dull yellowish green flowers that are odorless and without nectar. The cloud of pollen that floats up when the bush is shaken indicates that it is wind pollinated. When it bears seed, the bush is made conspicuous by the silver-colored silky tails of the fruits.

Thimbleberry (*Rubus deliciosus*). P. 17. When the pioneer naturalist Edwin James in 1820 discovered this plant in the Southern Rockies, he somehow got the idea that "the fruit is large and delicious". A later botanist corrected this with the observation, "flavor not agreeable to the human palate". The white, flat flowers are enormous—2 inches in diameter—compared with those of the closely related raspberries.

Chokecherry (*Prunus melanocarpa*). P. 18. An elegant bush with luxuriant, elongated clusters of white flowers that bloom in early summer and, by the end of July, become heavy bunches of reddish black berries. These are eaten by a variety of birds and mammals. Humans cannot eat large quantities of the raw berries because of the choking astringent substance they contain. This plant is often infested with "tent" caterpillars.

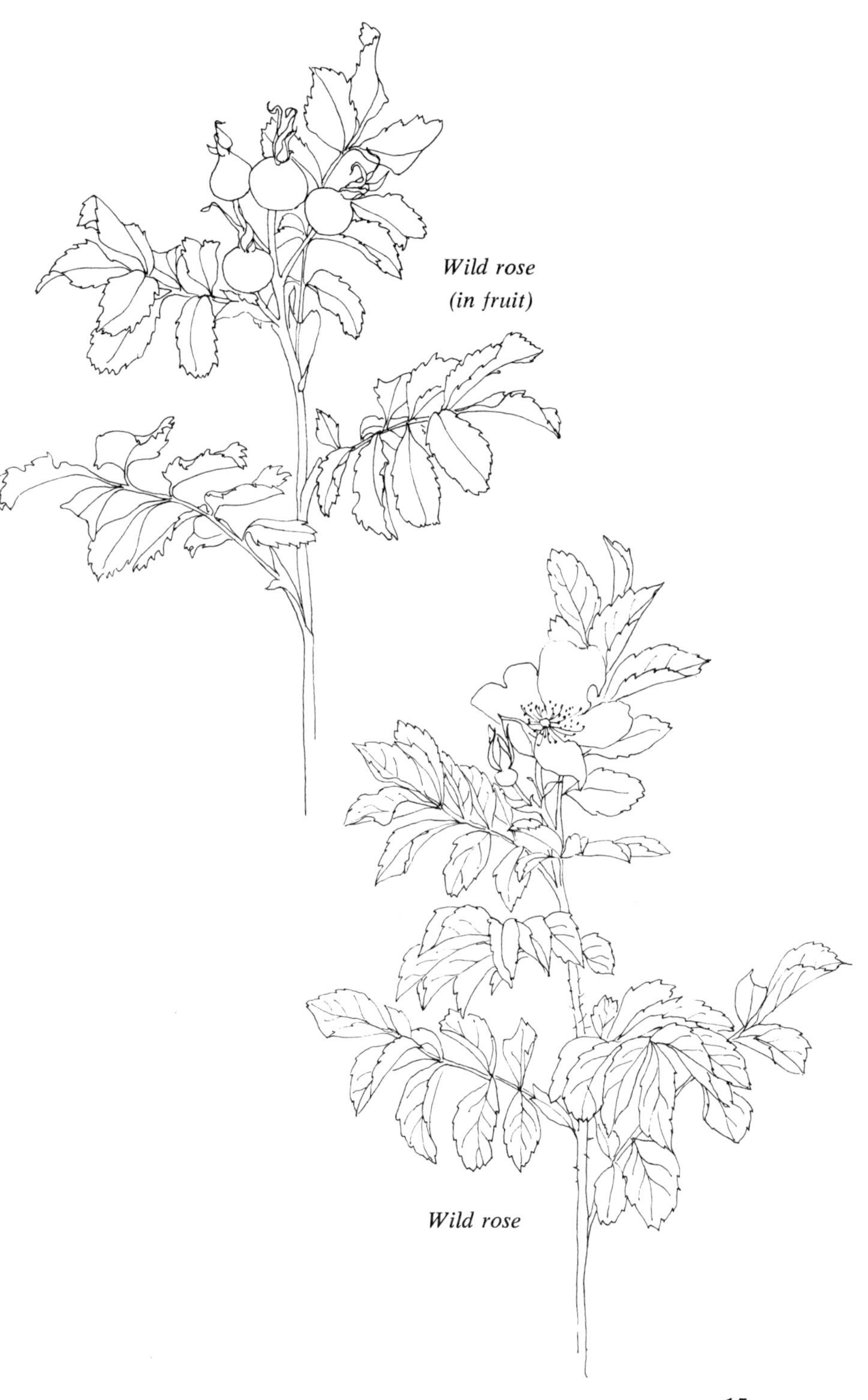

Wild rose
(in fruit)

Wild rose

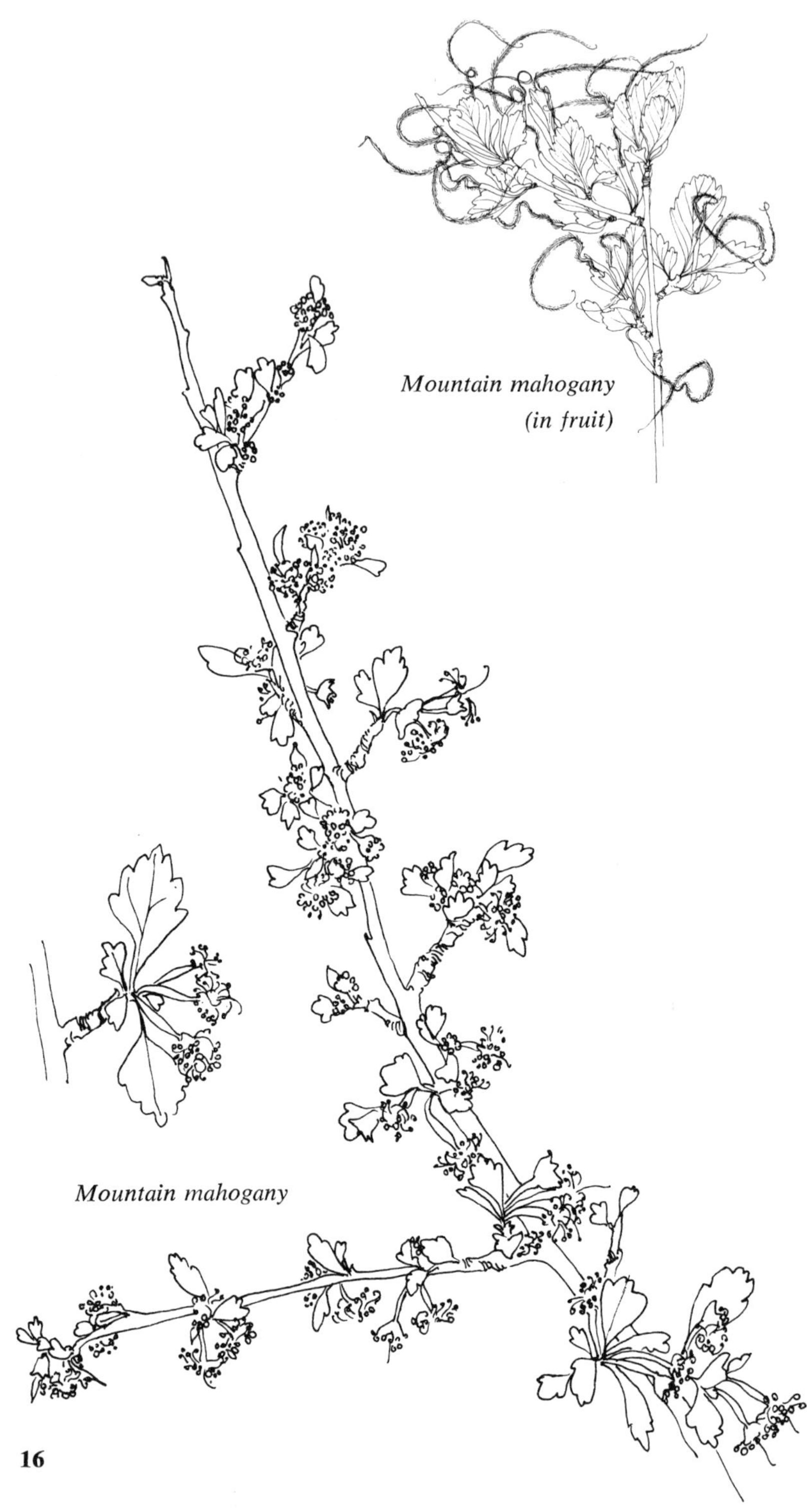

Mountain mahogany
(in fruit)

Mountain mahogany

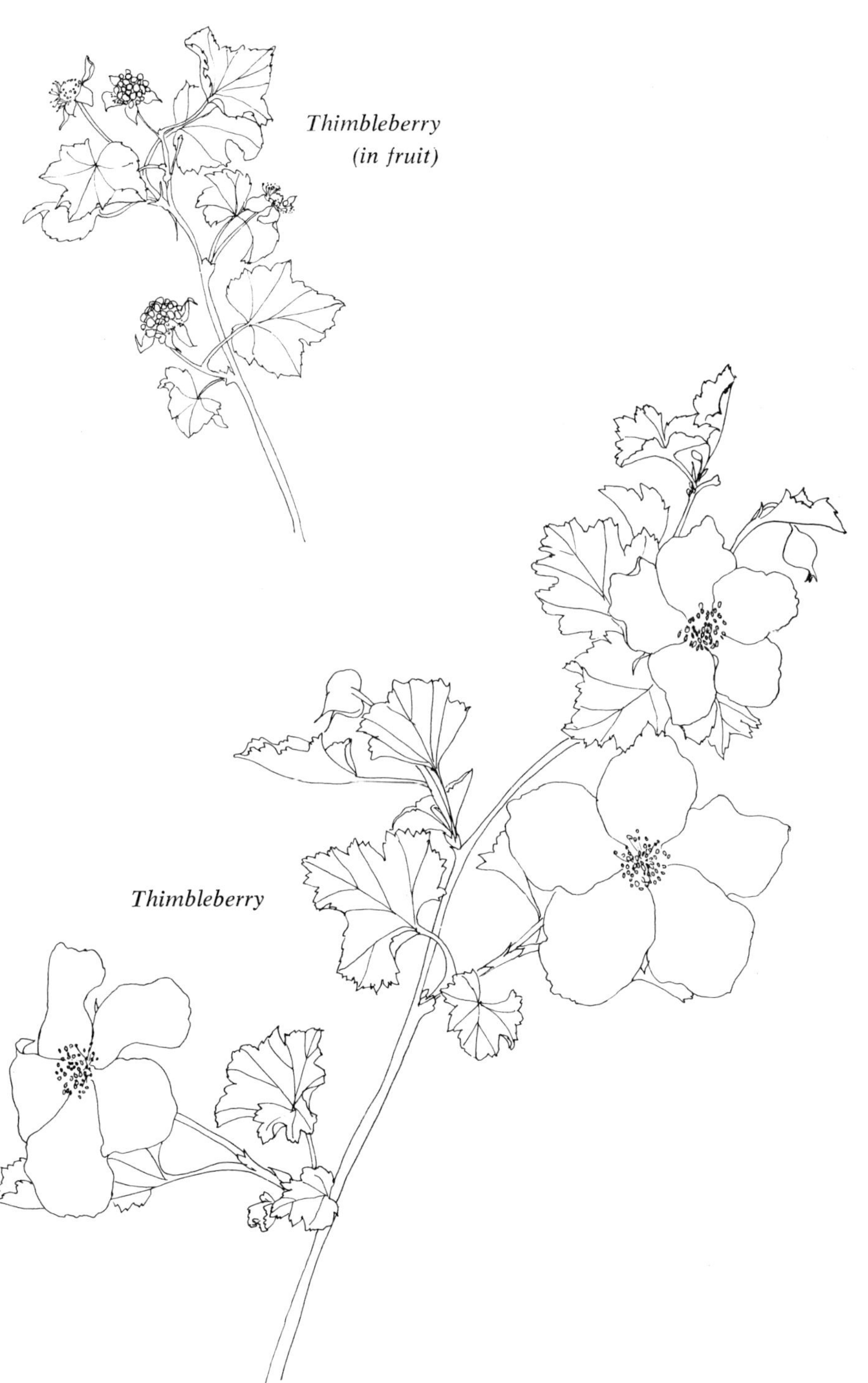

Thimbleberry
(in fruit)

Thimbleberry

Chokecherry
(in fruit)

Chokecherry

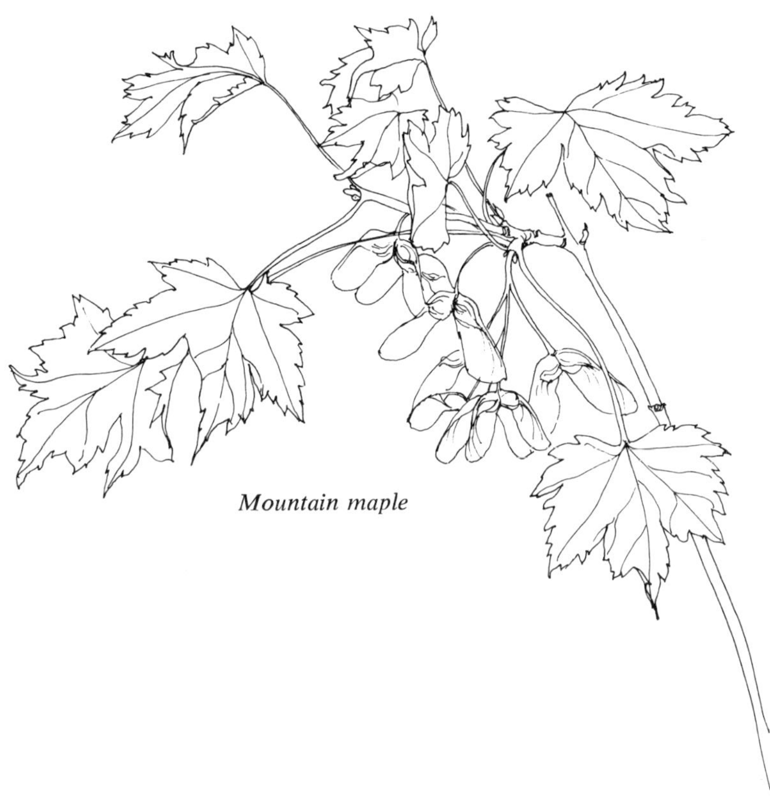

Mountain maple

Mountain maple (*Acer glabrum*). P. 19. A large, many-stemmed shrub found most commonly in the canyons and on their north slopes. The two-winged fruits often become bright red in mid-spring, before they mature. In fall the leaves turn the color of old, yellowed ivory.

Currants (*Ribes*). P. 20, 21. These bushes, which are especially common on the rough ground along the sides of the canyons, yield a rich crop of berries. The less common and more handsome species is the yellow-flowered Golden currant (*R. aureum*) with berries that are golden, red, or black, and appetizing. The more common species is the Wax currant (*R. cereum*) with dull pink flowers and red berries, bland-tasting when ripe, but said by some to taste like jasmine tea if picked when the dried flower is still attached.

Wax currant

Wax currant
(in fruit)

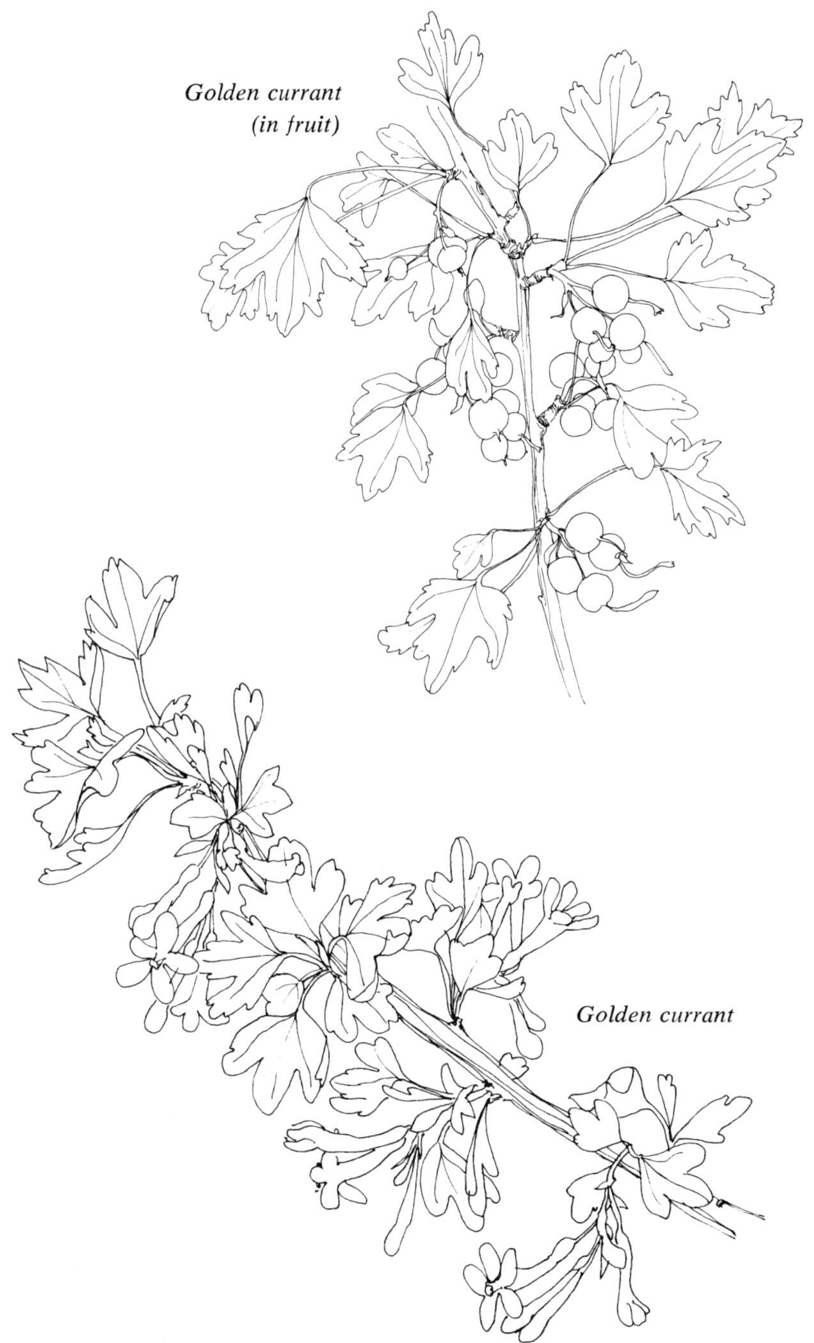

Golden currant
(in fruit)

Golden currant

Dwarf lead plant
Buckbrush

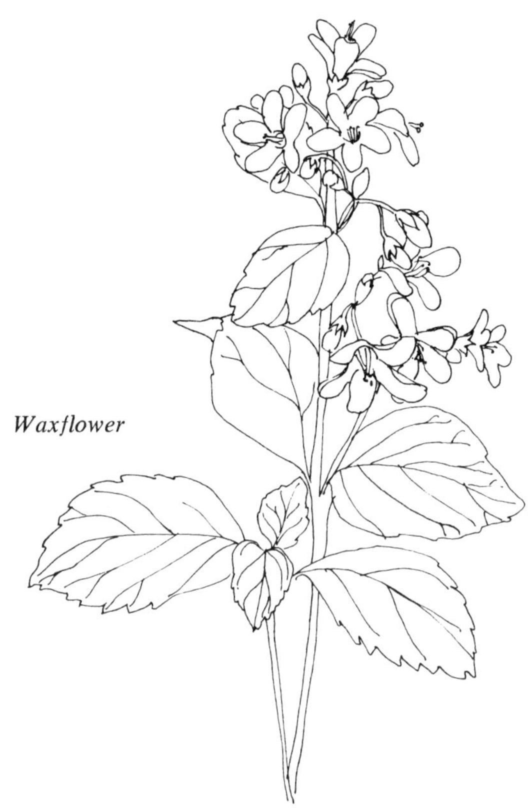

Waxflower

Buckbrush (*Ceanothus fendleri*). P. 22. A low, white-flowered, thorny bush found on dry, rocky hillsides. Closely related to New Jersey tea, which also occurs on the mesa, although not common.

Waxflower (*Jamesia*). P. 23. This medium-sized bush is frequently found, especially along the upper reaches of the mesa canyons. Each of the coarse saw teeth edging the leaves is rounded. The leaves are green above, frosted with silvery hairs on the underside. Flowers have white petals that are hairy on inner surface.

Dwarf lead plant (*Amorpha nana*). P. 22. A beautiful small shrub with heavy spikes of deep red-purple flowers. Scattered widely over the mesas from Skunk Canyon southward, but also locally abundant on these mesas, especially on north slopes. The drawing depicts only a stem of a bush. Its larger relative, *Amorpha fruticosa,* nearly head-high, is found along ditches, streamlets, and in seepages.

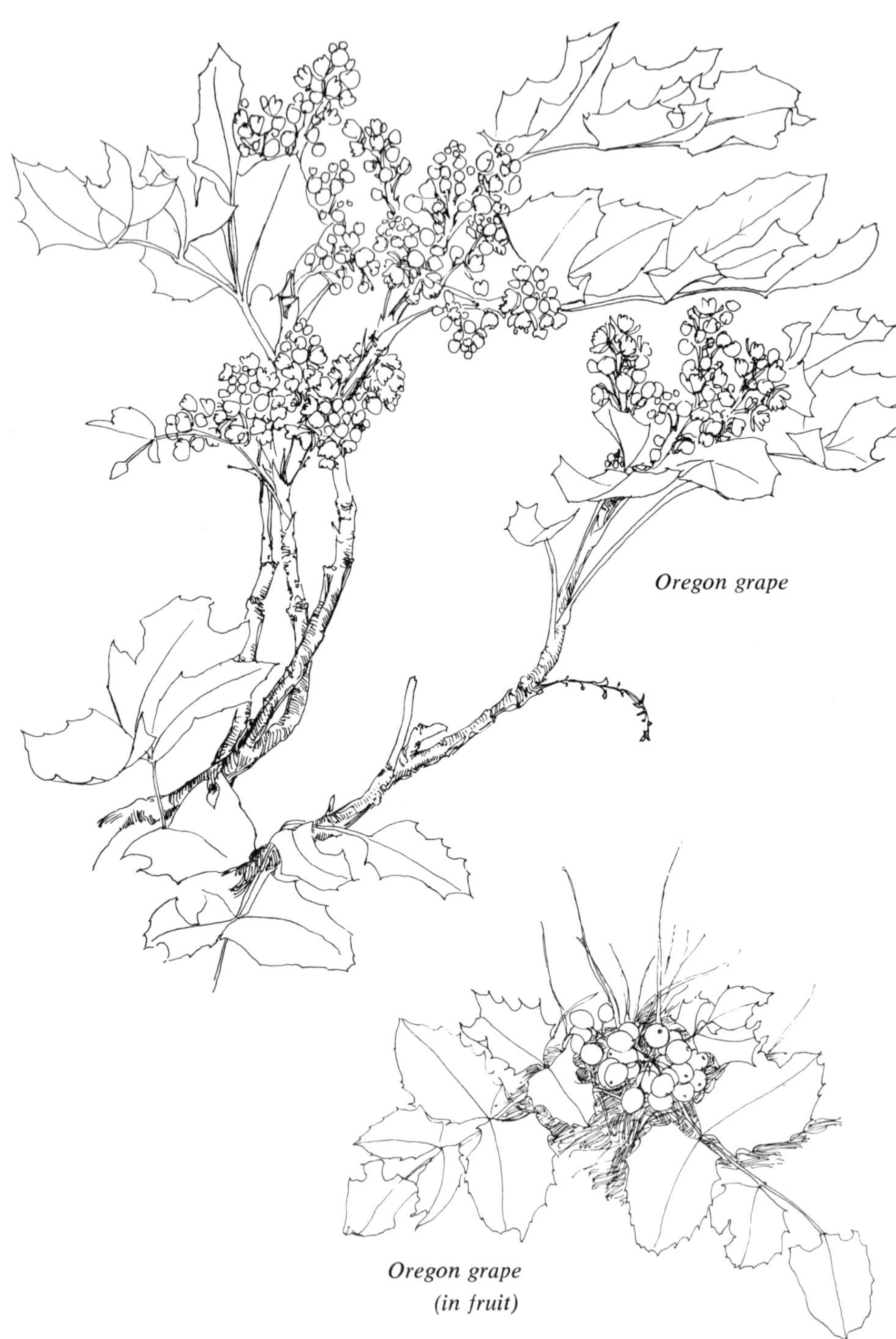

Oregon grape

Oregon grape
(in fruit)

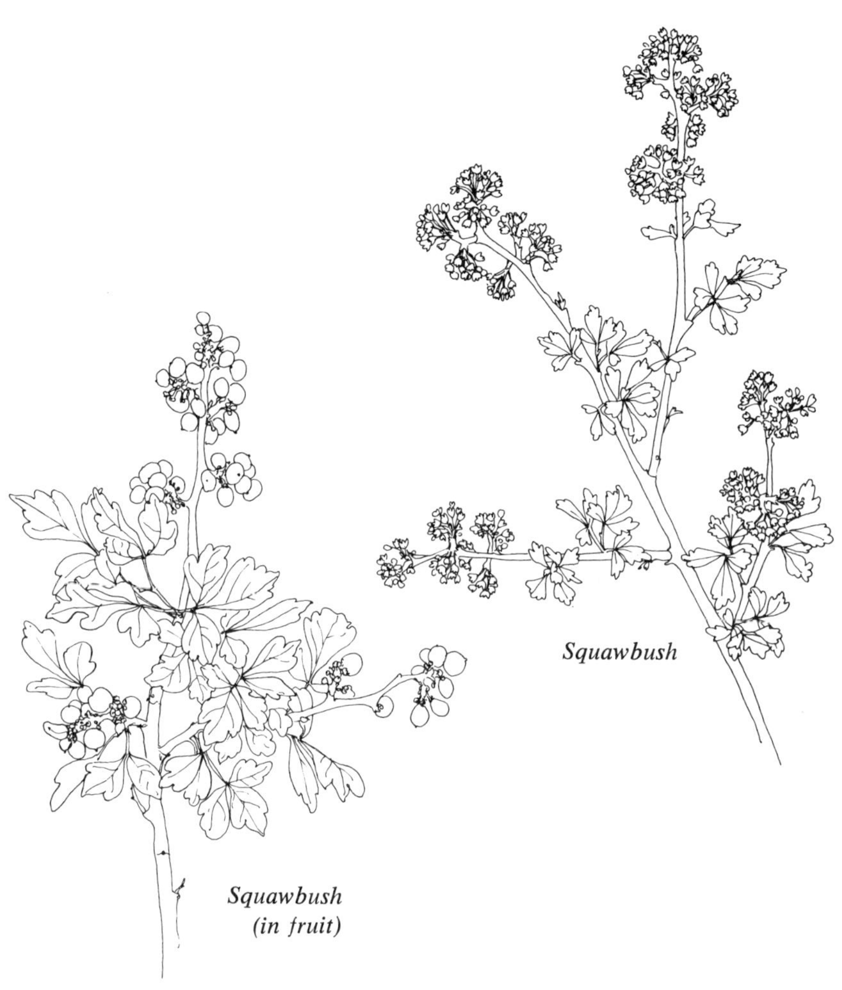

Oregon grape (*Mahonia repens*). P. 24. The evergreen leaflets (actually they are usually red by late winter) of this low shrub have the shape of Christmas holly leaves. It is a common plant, and the Concord grape-colored berries (edible for humans) is an important food supply for various animals. Flowers yellow.

Skunkbrush or squawbush (*Rhus trilobata*). P. 25. An abundant, medium-sized, tough and wiry bush. Its relationship to the sumac is shown by the red, fuzzy, sticky fruits that are a valuable contribution to the food supply of the birds of fall and winter. Small, yellow-green flowers.

Sumac

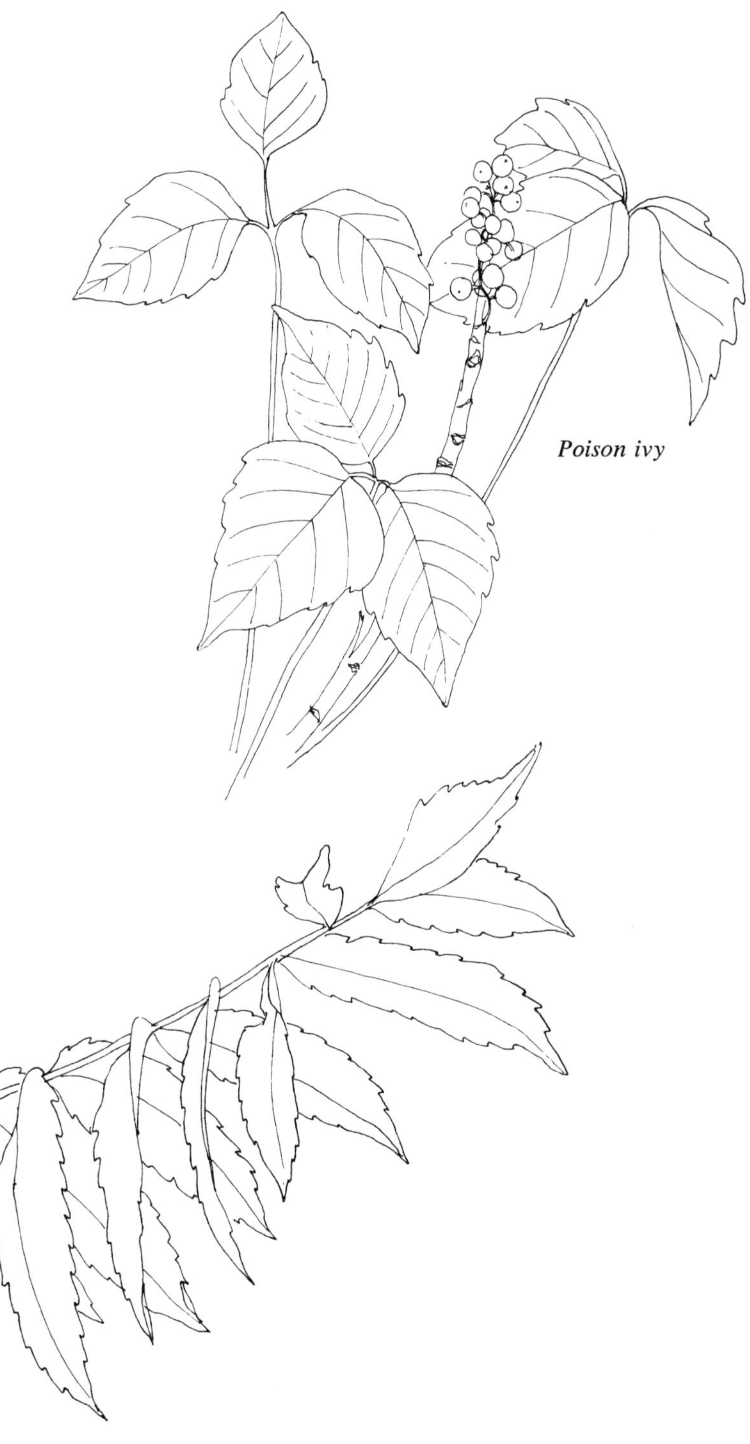

Poison ivy

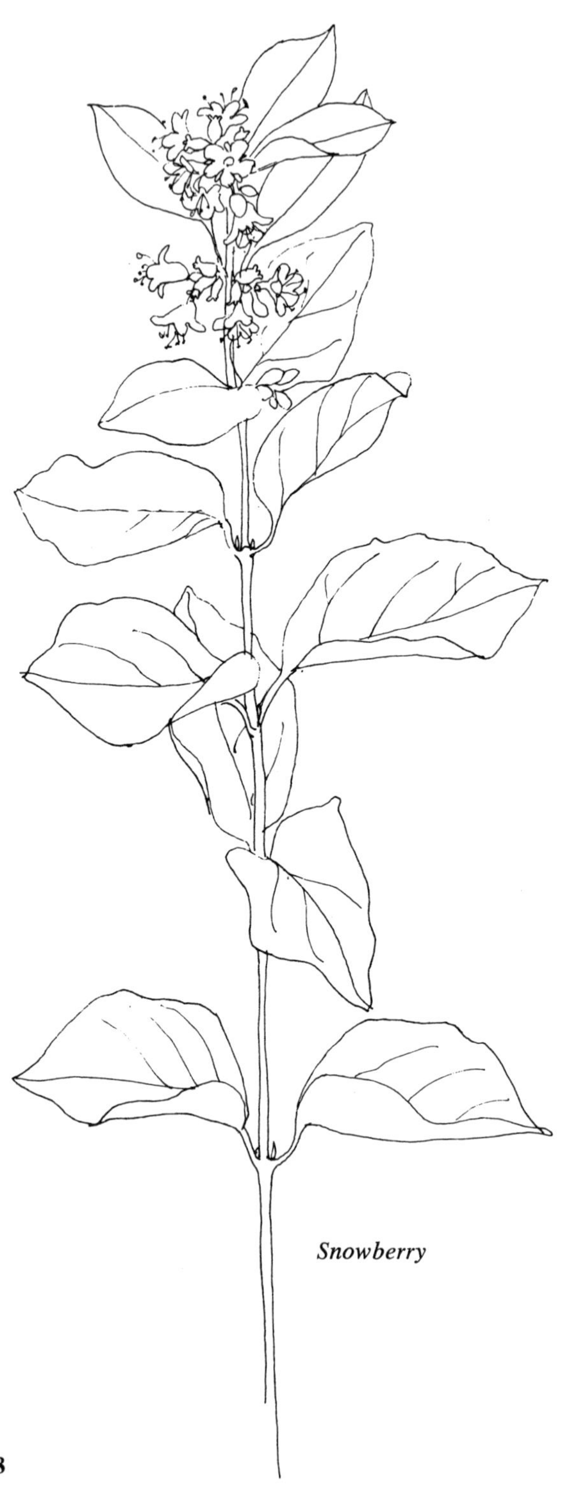

Snowberry

Virgin's bower

Sumac (*Rhus glabra*). P. 26. Similar to the garden Sumac, but smaller—about chest-high. Reproduces by runners and may form dense patches of a half-acre or more. The small greenish-yellow flowers are rich in nectar and pollen, and swarm with bees in the summer. The leaves are among the main contributors to the red fall colors of the floral landscape. The clusters of red, fuzzy fruits persist into winter and are an important food resource for wildlife.

Poison ivy. (*Toxicodendron radicans*). P. 27. If a person is one of those sensitive to the incredibly strong poison of this plant, which blisters the skin, he should condition himself to revulsion at the sight of the glossy, three-lobed leaves which usually lie close to the ground. The evil-looking gray winter stem and the waxy white berries also are poisonous. The small flowers are yellowish green.

Snowberry (*Symphoricarpos*). P. 28. Two common species of this relative of the honeysuckle provide much of the shrubby ground cover on the mesa. About knee-high. The berries are white, the flowers pink or white.

WOODY VINES

The woody vines are a part of the tangled vegetation of the mesa canyons and along South Boulder Creek. The Hop vine (*Humulus*), *Smilax,* and the Grape vine, *Vitis* (the grapes are edible, but minute by supermarket standards) are relatively uncommon. The most ubiquitous vine is Grandpa's whiskers or Virgin's bower (*Clematis ligusticifolia*), p. 29, a luxuriant plant that may almost smother small trees. In the late summer the abundant white flowers brighten up the canyons, and the clusters of long, silky white tails of the mature fruits (it is the female plants that are called "Grandpa's whiskers") are nearly as showy as the flowers.

SAGEBRUSH

The "real" sagebrush is *Artemesia tridentata,* which covers many hundreds of thousands of square miles in the West, but does not occur on the Enchanted Mesa. However, the Mesa does have two other species of *Artemesia*, with foliage of the same silvery color and ineffable odor, that are worth recognizing so that one can pick the leaves and sniff them. The Pasture sage (*A. frigida*) p. 31, is a low bush with a woody base. The crowded short leaves are so slender as to be almost thread-like. The other species, the Prairie sage (*A. ludoviciana*), p. 32, is not woody, and has fewer and wider leaves, that vary much in outline. Up in the pine forest, the leaves are more or less deeply cleft into several long points, while out on the grassland, well away from the trees, the leaves are "entire"; that is, not cleft or notched. There are all imaginable intermediates, so the two populations, that of the forest and the "prairie", must hybridize.

The inconspicuous flowers of *Artemesia,* that appear in late summer, are wind pollinated, and their abundant airborne pollen contributes much to hay fever.

The "sage" of the herb garden is not *Artemesia,* and is not related to it. *Artemesia,* especially in Europe, is called "wormwood". There, the aromatic oils of one of the species is a component of absinthe.

Pasture sage

Pasture sage

Prairie sage

Prairie sage

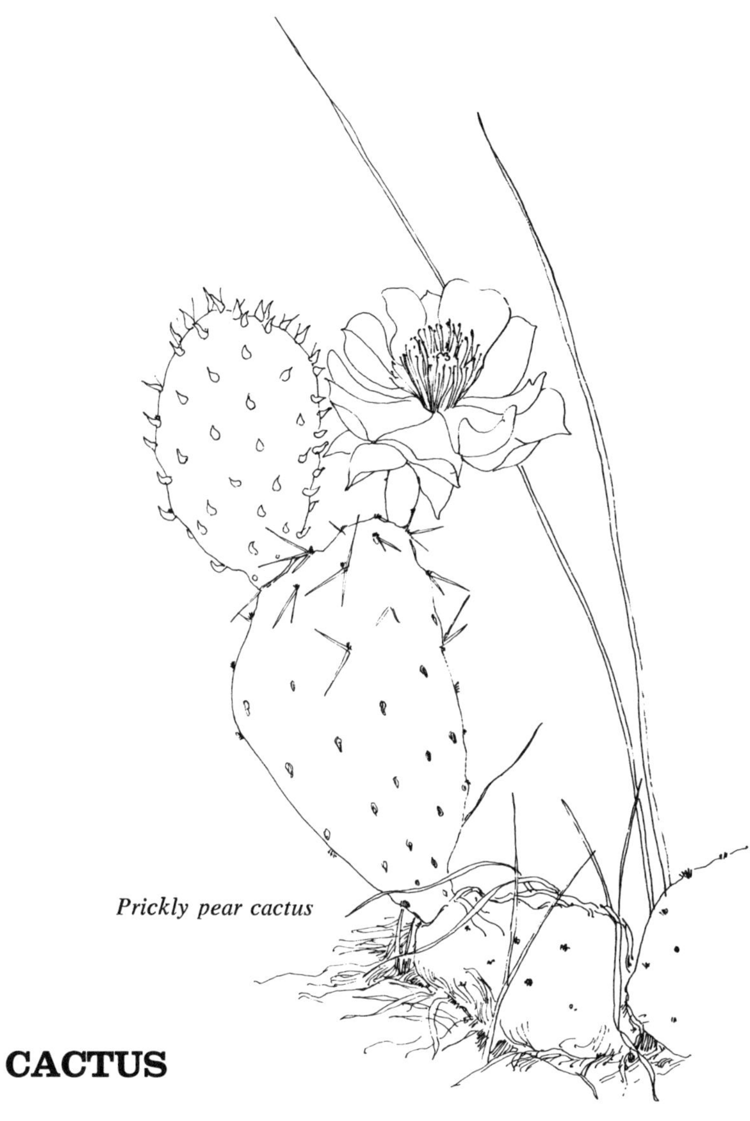

Prickly pear cactus

CACTUS

To continue the list of plants that are worth noting in their non-flowering stage, the common Prickly pear or Pad cactus on the mesa is *Opuntia compressa*, p. 33, which has few spines, as cacti go. The flowers are yellow. The purplish-red fruits are edible, but their clusters of microscopic spines are somewhat discouraging. The version of the ball cactus that is most common on the mesa is called "Hen-and-chickens" (*Echinus viridifloris*). The flowers are brownish to yellowish green.

GRASSES

Grasses are usually not included in the category "wild flowers" because their wind pollinated, complex flowers are small and not showy. There are many species, and their study is a demanding specialty. Most of the close-to-the-ground vegetation cover is of grass, a group of plants that protect themselves by producing, not spines or poisons, but hard spheres of quartz in their tissues, that wear out the teeth of all but a few kinds of animals with teeth that keep growing, to make up for the wear and tear of an all-grass diet.

Early in the spring an emerald carpet of new grass appears in the open pine forest, muting the sounds of the forest as a carpet does a barren house. By June, if there has been a rainy spring, the flowering stalks may be waist high. When the fruiting heads have developed, it will be seen that they appear to be the same as the heads of lawn grass let go to seed. That is, they are one or another species of blue grass, or *Poa*. These make up most of the ground cover of the forest, except in those dense stands of pine where only a few plants rise through the cover of dead pine needles.

There are a few of the many species of mesa grasses that should be mentioned here because they attract special attention for one reason or another. The Blue grama (*Bouteloua gracilis*), an important grass of the dry short-grass prairie, has a flowering head that is gracefully curved, with the fruits on one side of the stem, forming a narrow banner. The eye-catching heads of the Rattlesnake grass (*Bromus brizaeformis*) look very much like the rattle of the snake. The fruits of some of the grasses are collected by the hiker when he picks the "stickers" out of his socks. Most picturesque of these ankle-scratchers is the Needle grass (*Stipa*), with a long spiral tail fastened to the sharp-pointed fruit that is said to coil and uncoil with changes in humidity, forcing the seed into the ground as it does so.

WILDFLOWERS

To classify the wildflowers into categories of manageable size, we have divided them into two major groups by season—spring, which, contrary to astronomy, ends approximately when school is out (we take it as the end of May); and summer and fall, which make up the remaining flowering season. A number of plants do not fit neatly into this arbitrary classification so that, especially in late May and early June, one may have to look under both categories.

Within the seasonal categories, the flowers are further classified by color. It is difficult to draw lines in the color spectrum, and at the arbitrary boundaries that have been selected, again it may be necessary to look under two categories. Also, there is often individual variation, with flowers of the same species being pink or white, blue or pink, and so on.

Although this booklet is designed to provide recognition through overall appearance of the plant, rather than the minute details of flower structure described in the technical manuals, it is perhaps well to make a few general remarks about the flowers of those plants here called "wildflowers". The showy blooms have the function of attracting insects or, less commonly, hummingbirds. As these move from flower to flower, they transport pollen grains, which are minute male plants that grow on the receptive part (the stigma) of the female sex organ of the recipient plant and fertilize it.

Insects obtain food from flowers: the nectar, which is mainly a solution of sugar in water, and the protein-rich pollen grains themselves. The flowery brilliance of a mountain meadow is comparable to the dazzling display of neon lights on a city street lined with shops. The flowers are advertising for the attention of their customers (the insect pollinators) by means of color, pattern, and attractive odors.

Flowers have evolved many kinds of devices for making certain that pollen gets on to the stigma. It is the diversity of such biological inventions that accounts for most of the diversity of flowers. In a very general way, there are three kinds of flower structures that can be recognized at a glance. The primitive and regular flowers have all the petals alike and separate, and they have, at least very nearly, radial symmetry; examples are flowers of the cinquefoils, or of the Spring beauty. These often have a wide variety of insect pollinators. Or, in another type, the flower can be both regular and tubular. Here the petals, or petal equivalents, are fused together to form a more or less narrow tube. Examples are flowers of Puccoon or of Miner's candle. Flowers such as these may exclude many kinds of insects that do not have long tongues capable of reaching the nectaries at the bottom of the tube. Finally, there are irregular flowers, with only bilateral symmetry, and with the petals, or petal equivalents, differing from each other. Orchids are extreme examples of irregular flowers and may be fertilized by only one species of insect.

Among our wild flowers, various members of the legume group, such as Golden banner or the species of loco, are irregular. Such flowers tend to force the insect to use only the approaches to food sources that insure pollination, or actually have moving parts that are put into motion by the insect in such a way as to help bring about pollination.

A fourth type of "flower" is not, strictly speaking, a flower, but is a flower head. This is the composite "flower", characteristic of a group of plants with many species, some of them common, called the composites. Examples are the sunflower and dandelion. In the sunflower, each apparent petal is actually a long yellow flag, called a "ray", produced by a single extremely lopsided flower. The large central disc is a tightly-packed aggregation of hundreds of small complete flowers, each of which produces a seed. In the dandelion, all flowers of the head are about the same, so that there is little differentiation between a central disc and a peripheral set of rays.

Sticky cinquefoil

SPRING

FLOWERS YELLOW, ORANGE, ORANGE-RED, RED

Sticky cinquefoil (*Potentilla fissa*). P. 37. The common spring cinquefoil of the mesa. The name comes from the fact that many species, although not this, have leaves divided into five leaflets. Flowers yellow, regular, five-petalled.

Bladder pod (*Lesquerella montana*). P. 39. Common name comes from the shape of the fruit. Flowers yellow, regular, four-petalled. A crucifer (see under Candytuft, p. 64).

Whisk-broom parsley (*Harbouria trachypleura*). P. 42. The tiny regular yellow flowers make a good show because they are massed together into a number of umbrella-like structures. Late spring. This plant and its relatives form a group called the umbellifers.

Musineon (*Musineon divaricata*). P. 41. Again, the small yellow flowers of this umbellifer are conspicuous because they are massed, here into spherical clusters. Early spring.

False dandelion (*Microseris cuspidata*). P. 42. Leaves much different from those of the dandelion, shaped like wide grass blades, and with wavy, woolly margins. Yellow "flowers" composite; the globular fluffy seed heads snow-white.

Salsify, Oyster plant (*Tragopogon dubius*). P. 43. The lemon-yellow, composite flower heads are larger than those of the other dandelion-like wildflowers, and produce a tennis-ball size tawny, fluffy seed head. Leaves' like wide grass blades, but not woolly margined.

Arnica (*Arnica fulgens*). P. 44. This composite has brilliant yellow-orange flower heads. It is most abundant in May, and sometimes forms large patches in the meadows. By the beginning of summer the tawny, fluffy, dandelion-like seed heads, smaller than those of the Salsify, are a noticeable part of the landscape.

Dandelion (*Taraxacum officinale*). P. 45. A "wild" plant as well as one decorating lawns, and one of the earliest flowers of the mesa. The common name, which is altered French for "lion's tooth", refers to the jagged leaf margins.

Spring butterweed (*Senecio fendleri*). P. 46. A yellow composite with the small yellow flower heads in clusters, and a single main stem. The spring senecios of the mesa are extremely variable with respect to leaf shape and the webbiness of the lower leaves, and there may be more than one species involved.

Bladder pod
(with inset)

Whiskbroom parsley

Musineon

False dandelion

Salsify
(in fruit)

Salsify

Arnica

Dandelion

Frilled puccoon

Spring butterweed

Golden banner

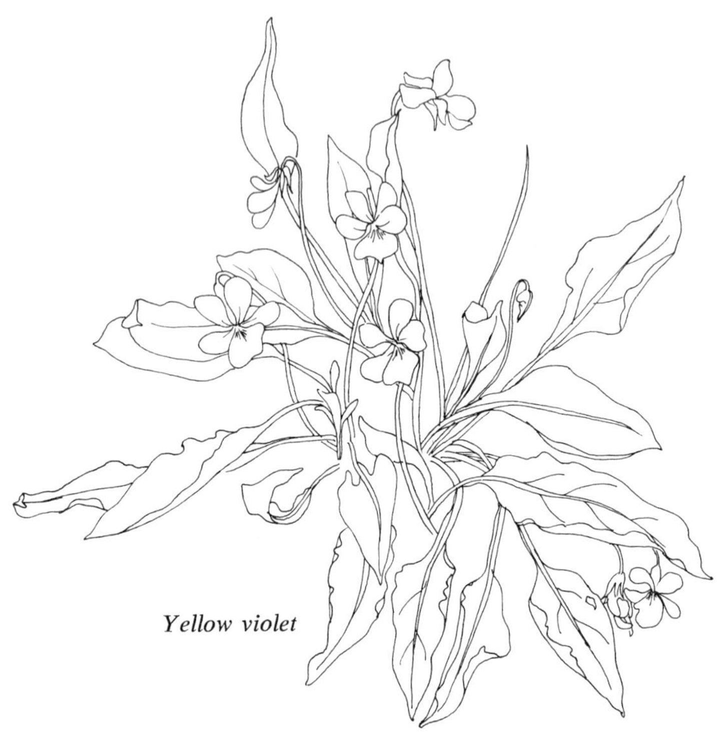

Yellow violet

Frilled puccoon (*Lithospermum incisum*). P. 46. Flowers yellow, tubular, regular; the lobes with frilled edges. The interesting-sounding common name is evidently from an old Virginian word meaning dye or stain. The roots are said to yield a red or purple dye.

Golden banner (*Thermopsis divaricarpa*). P. 47. This legume has the irregular flowers of that group. Flowers yellow. Lush foliage of three-fingered leaves. It is frequently infested with a large blue-back, soft-bodied beetle.

Yellow violet (*Viola nuttallii*). P. 48. The most common spring-flowering violet of the mesa. Grows singly rather than in patches.

Sheep sorrel (*Rumex acetosella*). P. 49. Although the flowers are small, they are abundant on the stem, and as they redden with age, make this a conspicuous plant that brightens the wet swales of the mesa. The leaves are pleasantly acidic to the taste.

Sheep sorrel

Erodium

FLOWERS PINK, MAGENTA

Spring beauty (*Claytonia rosea*). P. 51. This small, pinkish or white flower appears in early spring, and blooms for several weeks. The same species forms vast carpets of flowers in the eastern hardwood forests; here it is usually scattered. Flowers regular, with five separate petals.

Storksbill, Erodium (*Erodium cicutarium*). P. 50. With small, regular flowers, the petals bright rose. One of the first spring flowers, they even appear on mild days throughout much of the winter. When it goes to seed, a long beak protrudes from the flower, hence the common name.

Spring beauty

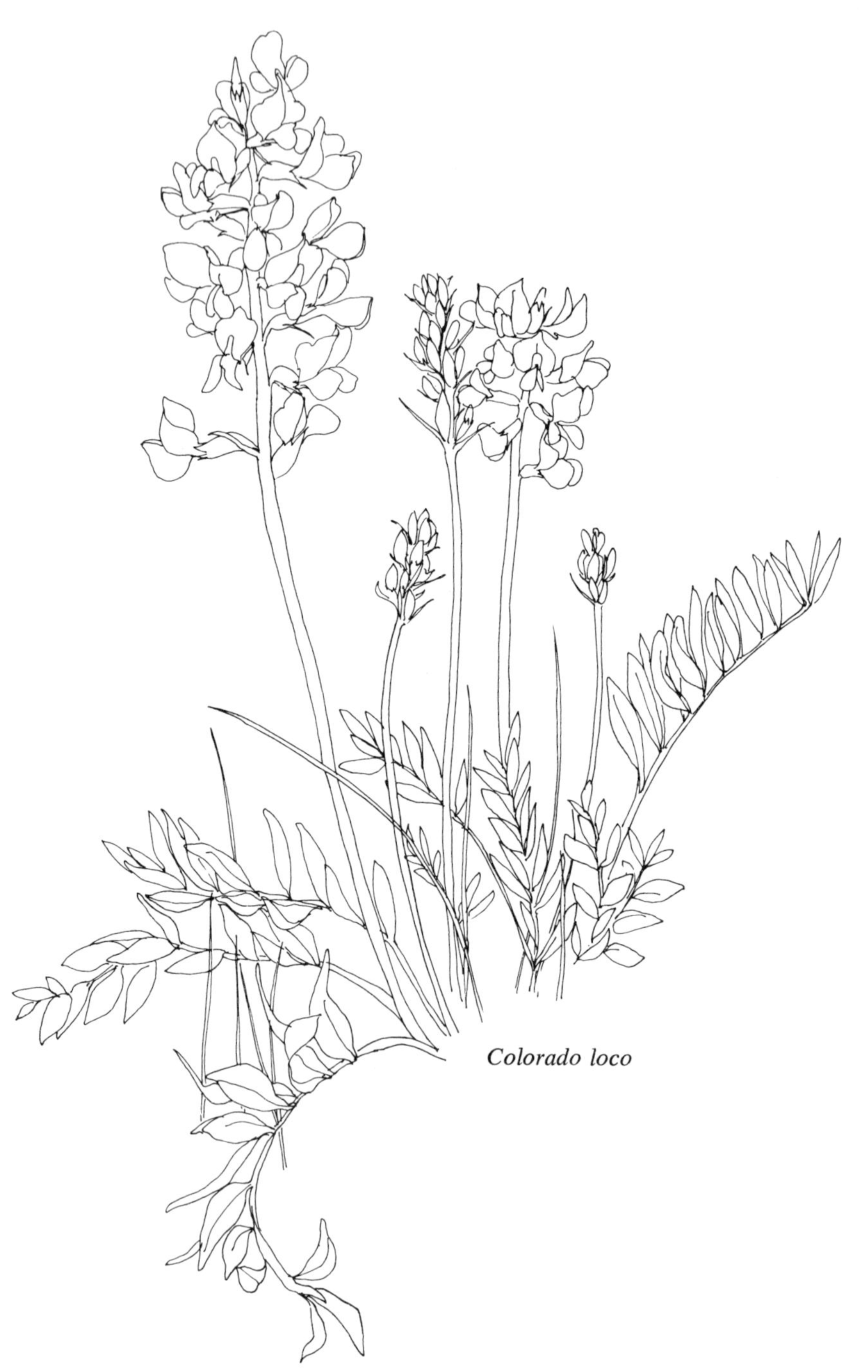

Colorado loco

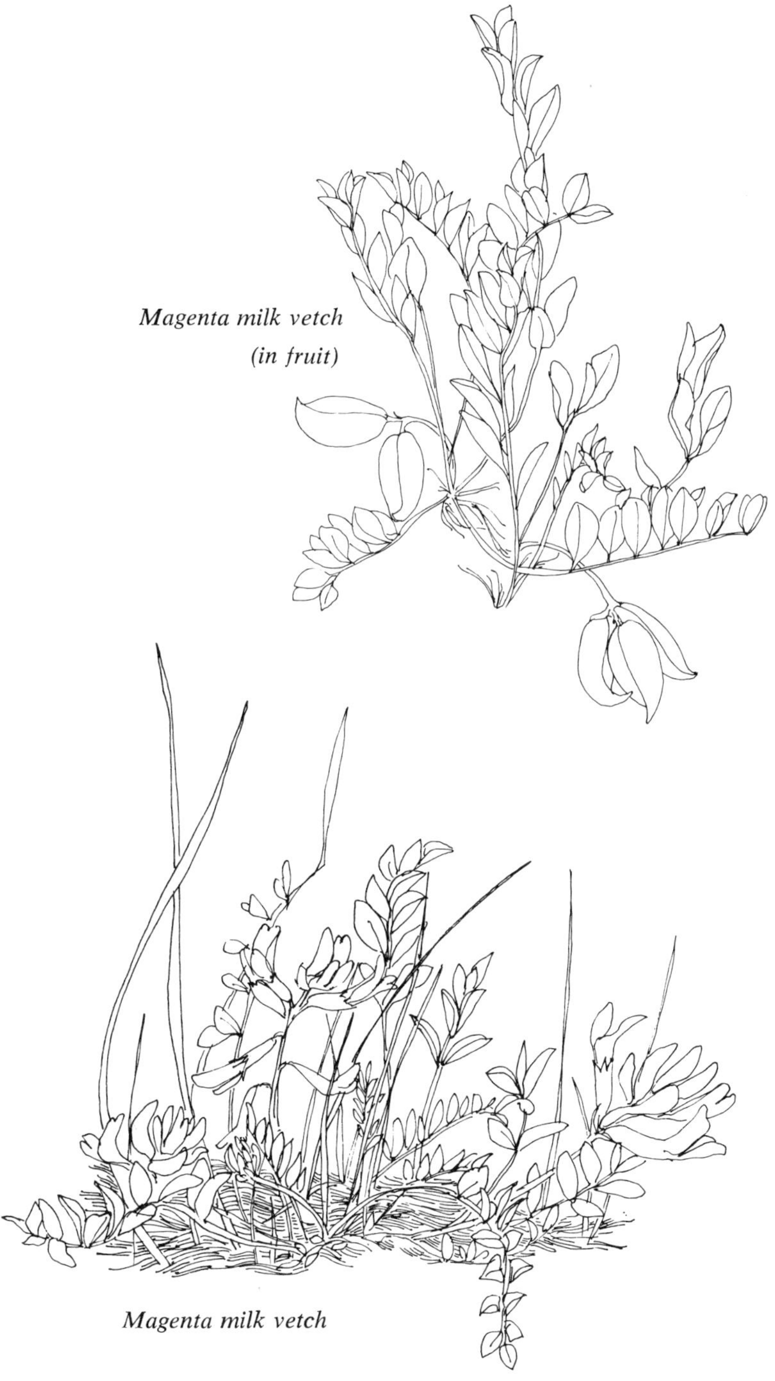

Magenta milk vetch
(in fruit)

Magenta milk vetch

Colorado loco (*Oxytropis lambertii*). P. 52. A conspicuous plant with masses of brilliant magenta blooms, common on the mesa in late spring. Flowers irregular (belongs to the legume group).

Magenta milk vetch (*Astragalus shortianus*). P. 53. Another legume, much smaller and more inconspicuous than the above, with irregular, magenta flowers. Leaflets silky. Mature seed pods large for the size of the plant. The innermost part of the flower, called the keel, is an oval envelope, slit open along one side, that contains the stamens and style. The species of *Astragalus* have the tip of the keel rounded. The locos (*Oxytropis*) have the tip sharply pointed.

Pussytoes (*Antennaria rosea*). P. 54. This composite flower is constructed of innumerable translucent, parchment-like scales tightly packed together so as to more or less resemble soft kitten-paws; they vary in color from pink to white. The flowering stalks grow up from a dense mat of woolly leaves.

Pussytoes

FLOWERS LAVENDER, PURPLE, BLUE

Pasque flower (*Pulsatilla patens*). P. 56, 57. The quiet beauty of this plant, and its gallant appearance early in the spring, when many frosty and snowy nights still lie ahead, make it a favorite. The large lavender-white flowers are regular.

Chiming bells (*Mertensia lanceolata*). P. 58. A common spring flower, from streamside to the forests of the mesa tops. Flowers regular, tubular; buds pink, flowers frosty blue.

Purple milk vetch (*Astragalus agrestis*). P. 59. This small *Astragalus* (see p. 59) has the magenta flowers clustered into rather compact heads; leaflets small, not silky.

Vetch (*Vicia americana*). P. 60. A legume, with irregular flowers; leafy stems tipped with tendrils. Late spring, early summer. Flowers vary from pink through purple to blue.

Baby blue-eyes (*Collinsia parviflora*). P. 59. A very small plant most likely discovered when one's eyes are near ground level; lives back in the forest shade, or damp places in the grassland. Leaves purple underneath. Flowers irregular, predominantly blue.

Purple larkspur (*Delphinium nelsonii*). P. 61. A dwarf plant, compared to most garden larkspurs; flowers in late spring and early summer. The purple flowers are irregular.

Early blue penstemon (*Penstemon virens*). P. 61. The first and most abundant of the penstemons, also flowers well into the summer. Leaves small and bright green, flowers blue. Flowers irregular, like the garden snapdragon, whose jaws open and shut when the base of the flower is squeezed.

Pasque flower

Pasque flower
(in fruit)

Chiming bells

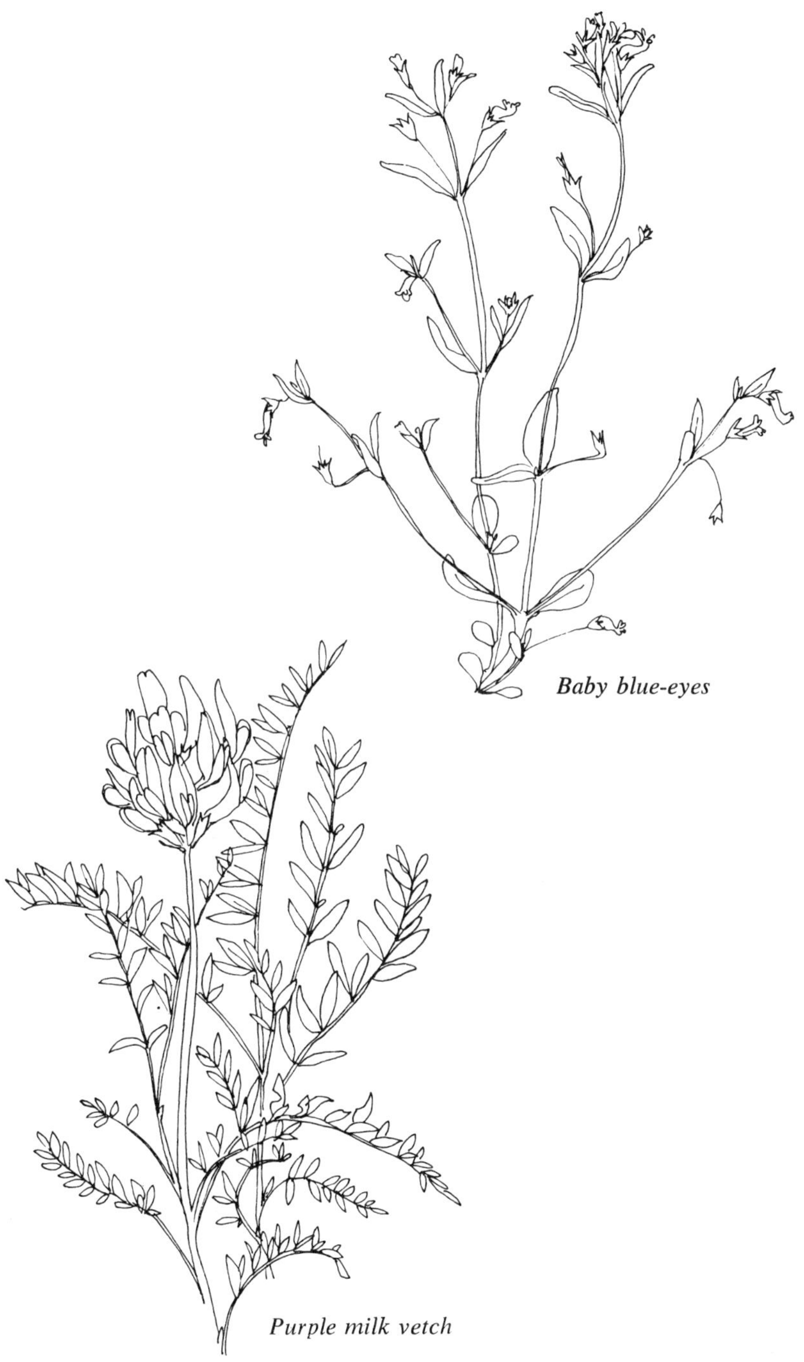

Baby blue-eyes

Purple milk vetch

Vetch

Purple larkspur

Early blue penstemon

Birds-foot violet (*Viola pedatifolia*). P. 62. This somewhat uncommon violet is striking on account of the large blue flowers. Named for the shape of the leaves, unusual for a violet. Often grows at the base of large boulders. As with all violets, the flowers are irregular.

Heartsease, Field pansy (*Viola kitaibeliana*). P. 62. A small annual violet, related to the garden pansy. Locally abundant on south slopes fed by seepage from the gravel-clay contact near the top of the mesa. The extra leaves at the base of the true leaves ar distinctive. Flowers usually some shade of blue or purple, but sometimes creamy white.

FLOWERS WHITE OR OFF-WHITE

Candytuft (*Thlaspi montanum*). P. 62. A crucifer, like *Lesquerella* (p. 39). The generally small flowers of this group have four petals, which gives the name (crucifer, or cross-bearer.) The fruit grows upward from the center of the flower, becoming relatively large, green (providing a significant photosynthetic surface), and appearing in a variety of shapes.

Only one other group of conspicuous mesa wildflowers is 4-petalled. This is the evening primrose group, in which the long, slender fruit appears below the flower.

Most crucifers have small, inconspicuous flowers, and there is a host of such species, here mainly ignored, on the mesa. They are especially abundant as weeds on the disturbed ground of the roadsides, and in overgrazed pastures, but there are also many obscure native species of interest to the specialist. The candytuft is mentioned on account of its pure white flowers that appear in the forest early in the spring, when there are few flowers about. A small, delicate plant.

Penny-cress (*Thlaspi arvense*). P. 64. Another spring crucifer with small white flowers, but the fruits become relatively immense coin-shaped structures that are often used in dry-weed bouquets.

Mouse-ear (*Cerastium arvense*). P. 65. A dominant spring flower of the mesa. Flowers white, regular, open; the plant less than a foot high.

Chickweed (*Stellaria jamesiana*). P. 66. A relative of the mouse-ear; not very common, generally occurring in shaded, damp places.

Salt and pepper (*Lomatium orientale*). P. 66. A low, early-flowering umbellifer (a group of plants including *Musineon*, p. 41, and *Harbouria*, p. 40) whose very small flowers are grouped into tight, many-flowered clusters that have the color of a mixture of salt and pepper.

Penny-cress
Candytuft

Mouse-ear

Salt and pepper
Chickweed

Sticky gilia, Spike gilia (*Ipomopsis spicata*). P. 68. The small flowers are regular and tubular. Generally single stemmed, hence the name, but sometimes with several stems branching from the base. When grasped firmly, the whole plant feels sticky.

Creamy milk vetch (*Astragalus drummondii*). P. 69. A common legume which forms large patches of yellowish-white flowers on the hillsides of the mesa, late spring to early summer. Leaves hairy.

White larkspur (*Delphinium virescens*). P. 68. A common late spring and early summer flower. Flowers irregular.

Pussytoes (*Antennaria*). See under Spring—pink flowers.

White violet (*Viola rugulosa*). P. 70. Grows in patches, usually in shady places.

Easter daisy (*Townsendia hookeri*). P. 70. One of the earliest plants to flower on the mesa. The one or more white, daisy-like flower heads, scarcely one inch in diameter, are stemless, being embedded in a cushion of narrow, densely packed gray-green leaves.

Sand lily (*Leucocrinum montanum*). P. 71. The long-tubular, regular, and six-lobed flowers rise directly from the ground, without a visible stem. The pure white flowers brighten up the relatively monotonous mesa slopes of earliest spring.

Death camus (*Zygadenus venosus*). P. 71. A lily with regular 6-lobed flowers. Very poisonous.

Spring beauty. See under Spring—pink flowers.

Sticky gilia

White larkspur

Creamy milk vetch

White violet
Easter daisy

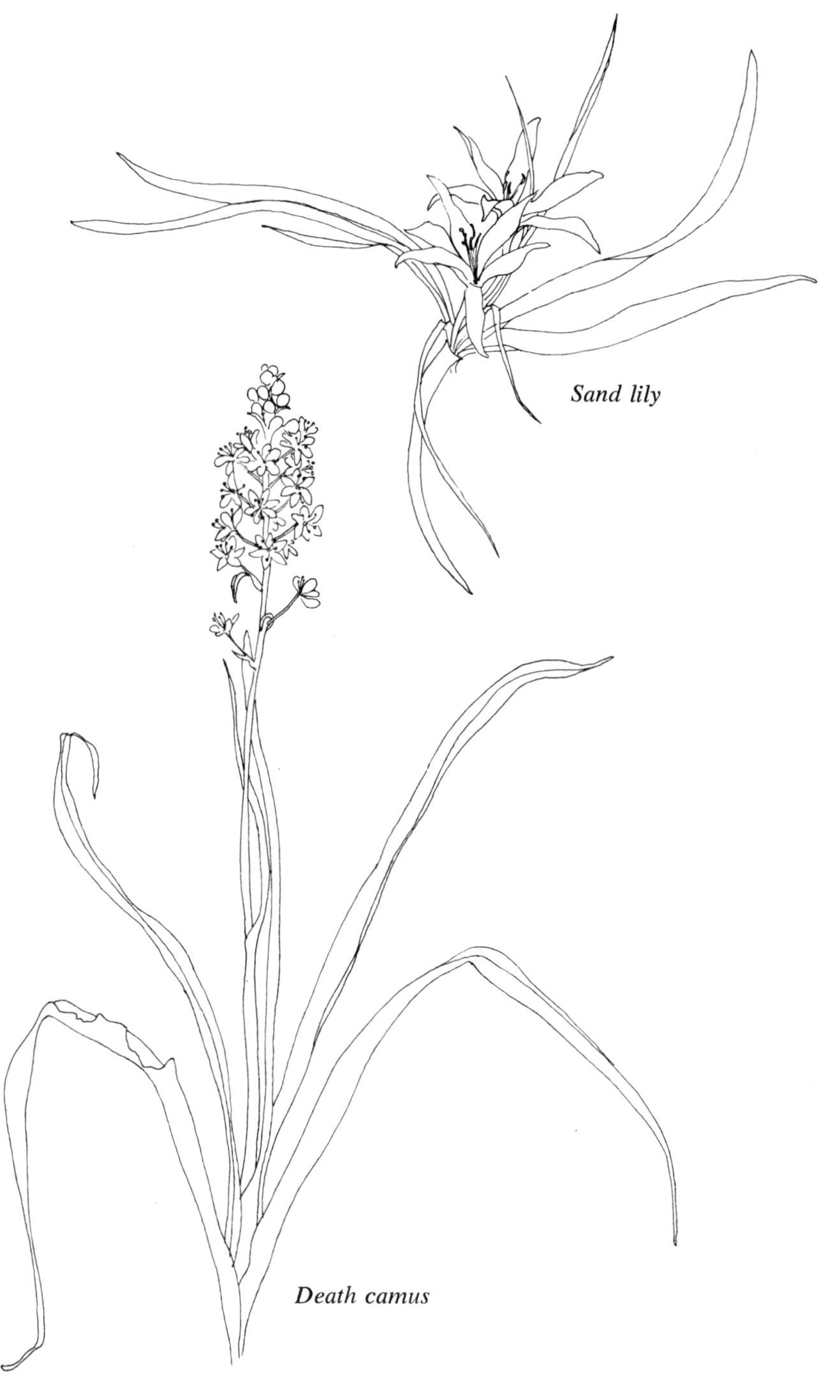

Sand lily

Death camus

SUMMER · FALL

FLOWERS YELLOW, ORANGE, RED-ORANGE, RED

Wallflower (*Erysimum asperum*). P. 73. A showy crucifer, with crowded clusters of relatively large flowers ranging in color from yellow to orange.

Five-fingered cinquefoil (*Potentilla gracilis*). P. 74. This mesa cinquefoil is variable in leaf pattern on account of hybridizing with another common mesa species, the Woolly or Silverleaf cinquefoil (*P. hippiana*), p. 74. Petals pastel yellow, with the centers more brilliant.

Tall sulfur flower (*Eriogonum alatum*). P. 75. Flowers and fruits small, inconspicuous, greenish-yellow. Leaves and flowers sparse, but plant as much as five feet tall, common, and in late summer looks like fencerows on the skyline of distant mesas.

Sulfur flower (*Eriogonum umbellatum*). P. 75. A low plant with small yellow flowers crowded together into bright clusters.

Stonecrop (*Sedum lanceolatum*). P. 76. The yellow flowers small but massed to make a showy cluster. Leaves "succulent" (thick, short, and presumably well-stuffed with water) and close to the ground.

Klamath weed (*Hypericum perforatum*). P. 76. Flowers fairly large and showy, but the off-color yellow, perhaps caused by the black dots along the edges of the petals, gives the plant a somewhat dowdy look.

When the small leaves are held up to the sky, they are seen to be dotted with small transparent windows. The weed, poisonous to livestock, has long been established in huge masses west of Rocky Flats, where it has been partially held in check by a small blue beetle purposely introduced to feed on it. Within the past ten years it has appeared on the Enchanted Mesa, and becomes more common and more northerly year by year.

Wallflower

Five-fingered cinquefoil

Woolly or
Silverleaf cinquefoil

Tall sulfur flower

Sulfur flower

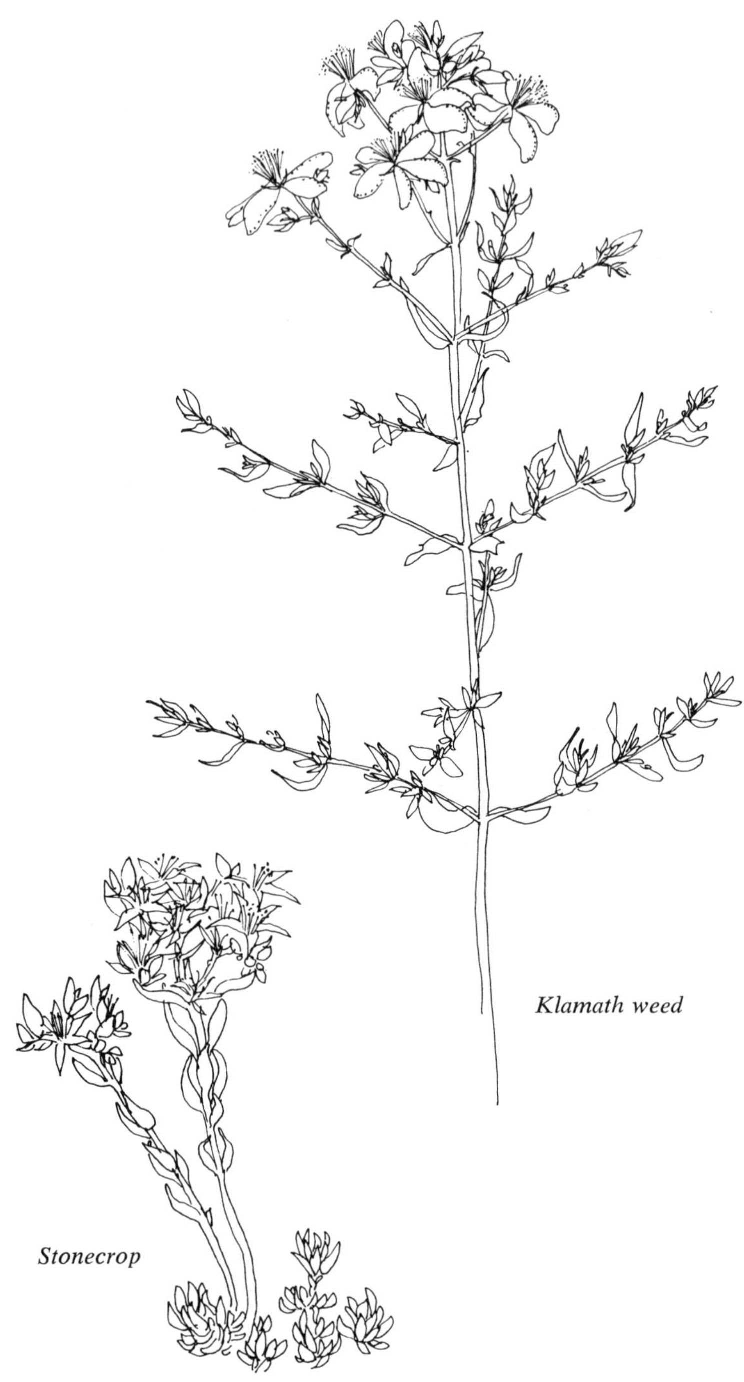
Klamath weed
Stonecrop

Copper mallow

Wood sorrel (*Oxalis dillenii*). P. 78. This small yellow-flowered plant with creased clover-like leaves has a refreshingly sour taste caused by the contained oxalic acid, a chemical that is poisonous in large quantities.

Copper mallow (*Sphaeralcea coccinea*). P. 77. This small plant has regular flowers with separate petals of a color unlike that of any other plant in the area—a clear coppery-scarlet. Mainly on dry ground at the lower ends of the canyons.

Wood sorrel

*Stemless yellow
evening primrose*

Evening primrose

Yellow stemless evening primrose (*Oenothera brachycarpae*). P. 78. Large, floppy, regular yellow flowers, close to the ground.

Evening primrose (*Oenothera strigosa*). P. 79. A tall, bushy plant, two or three feet high, with the yellow flowers rather small for an *Oenothera*. Pollinated by a strange, small bee that flies in early dawn, furnished with special pollen brushes to handle the large pollen grains that come in strings, and with large ocelli ("simple" eyes) for use in the dim light.

Puccoon (*Lithospermum multiflorum*). P. 81. Unlike the spring Puccoon, this species has the lobes of the yellow flowers smooth, rather than frilled.

Buffalo bur (*Solanum rostratum*). P. 82. This near relative of the potato was the preferred food of the famed Colorado potato beetle, until the early settlers took up farming in the Rocky Mountain west. The regular, wide-tubular flowers are yellow; the fruit is described in one manual of botany as "horridly prickly".

False salsify (*Scorzonera laciniata*). P. 83. Now one of the commonest flowers of late spring and early summer along roadsides and other disturbed areas, this plant was unknown in the region little more than a decade ago. It is a native of Europe. The flower heads of *Scorzonera* fold up by midday.

Prickly lettuce (*Lactuca scariola*). P. 84. A tall scraggly plant with small yellow flower heads and leaves with prickles on the underside of the midrib. Leaves with a tendency to orient themselves in a north-south direction.

Sunflower (*Helianthus annuus*). P. 85. An annual that becomes abundant on freshly disturbed ground, then, in a few years, disappears because of changing soil conditions. Flower head with dark center.

Perennial sunflowers (*Helianthus rigidus*). P. 86. (*H. pumilus*). P. 87. These sunflowers of the undisturbed ground grow in clumps or short rows. The center of the flower head of the first is brown, the second, yellow.

Goldenrod (*Solidago pallida*). P. 87. A composite with small flower heads, clustered into a showy yellow mass that attracts many kinds of insects who search for pollen and nectar.

Cone flower (*Ratibida columnifera*). P. 88. As with the sunflowers, the rays of this composite may have a rare genetic mutation that makes them maroon instead of the normal yellow.

Puccoon

Buffalo bur

False salsify

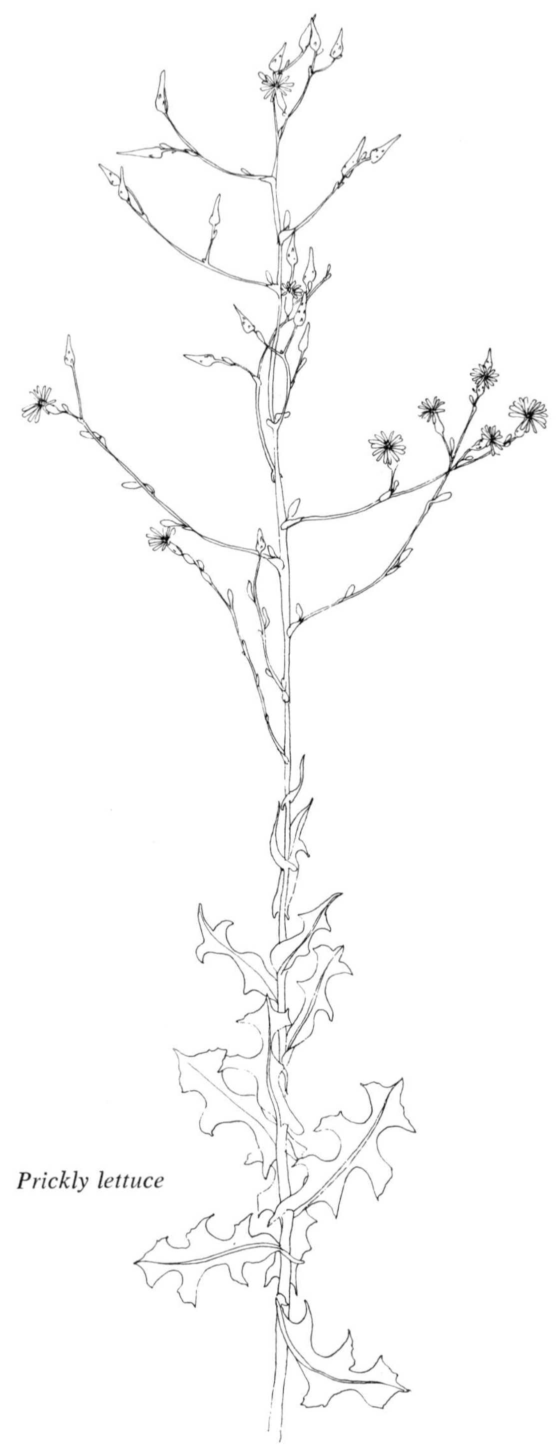

Prickly lettuce

Annual sunflower

Perennial sunflower

Perennial sunflower

Goldenrod

Cone flower

Gaillardia (*Gaillardia aristata*). P. 90. The same species is grown in the garden, where it is sometimes called the Blanketflower. Even in the wild it is variable, with the rays varying in shape, length, and in color from yellow to orange. The center of the flower head is generally a deep reddish-purple. Leaves are sometimes smooth-margined, sometimes toothed.

Golden aster (*Heterotheca*). A common, low yellow composite with several flower heads on each stem. Early in the summer flower heads are smaller and more widely separate; later, plants appear that have larger heads crowded closely together. This apparently is the result of the seasonal distribution of two species, the earlier *H. horrida* (p. 91) and the later *H. villosa* (p. 91).

Tall butterweed (*Senecio spartioides*). P. 92. Unlike the other common *Senecio* on the mesa (the single-stalked *S. fendleri*), this is a tall, many-branched plant whose scattered yellow flower heads make it an important part of the late summer and early fall landscape.

Gumweed (*Grindelia squarrosa*). P. 93. A late summer yellow composite with the flower heads very sticky on the underside; plants with a resinous, aromatic odor. Especially common in disturbed soil. A closely related species is said to reach its lower limit on the mesa, and extend on up into the subalpine.

Snakeweed (*Gutierrezia sarothrae*). P. 93. This low, bushy, somewhat woody composite, with abundant small yellow flower heads, is the last of the abundant species of wildflowers to be killed by the heavy freezes of autumn. It usually grows in clumps.

Great mullein (*Verbascum thapsus*). P. 94. An unmistakable plant, with its heavy flowering stalk rising to as much as five feet or more. Flowers yellow, slightly irregular, and blooming at intervals during summer and fall. The plentiful supply of seeds, still in place in capsules on the stalk, provide food for a number of kinds of birds well into the winter. It is also infested with swarms of a small black weevil.

Gaillardia

Late golden aster

Early golden aster

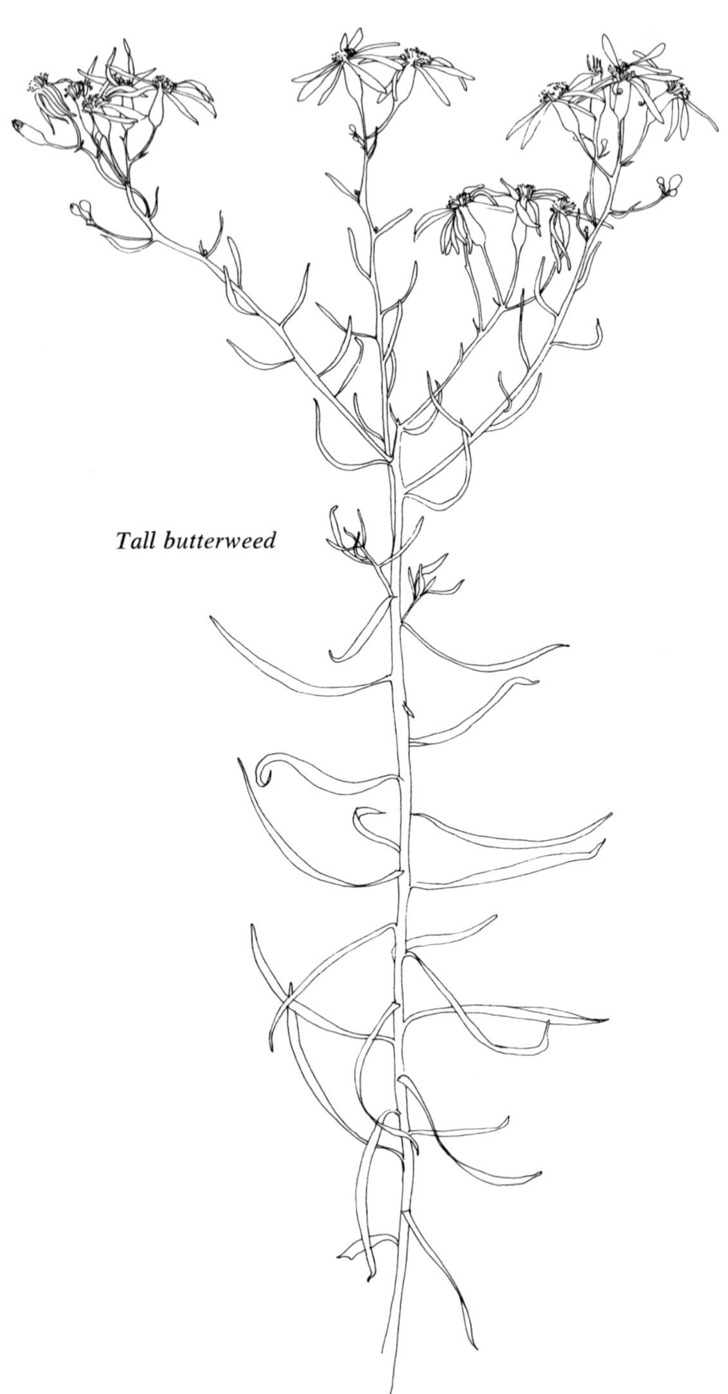

Tall butterweed

Gumweed
Snakeweed

Scarlet paintbrush

Great mullein

Scarlet paintbrush (*Castilleja minata*). P. 94. Colorado is one of the world's centers of diversity for castillejas. This scarlet species is common in the mountains, reaching the lower limit of its distribution on the south slopes of Skunk Canyon, near NCAR, and Cemetery Gulch. A few miles south of the Enchanted Mesa, a different, brilliantly reddish-orange species is at the northern limit of its range. A common, earlier species of paintbrush on the Enchanted Mesa is the low, inconspicuous *C. sessiliflora,* with dingy yellow flowers. The flowers of the paintbrushes are strongly irregular.

FLOWERS PINK, PURPLE-RED, PURPLE, LAVENDER, BLUE

Wild geranium (*Geranium fremontii*). P. 96. Does not look much like the geranium of the flower pot, which is not a true geranium, belonging to a different genus. In all but the driest summers, this is an exuberantly flowering bushy plant, about knee-high. Flowers pink to light purple.

Wild flax (*Linum lewisii*). P. 97. The fragile, sky-blue flowers make this an appealing wildflower.

Gaura (*Gaura*). These flowers show their relationship to the evening primroses by having 4-petalled flowers, with the fruit below the flower, and by the fact that they are visited by bees that fly in the dusky light of dawn or sunset. The spidery, long-stamened flowers are pinkish white to red, darkening with age. There are two species, the waist-high Tall gaura (*G. parviflora*), with stone-hard fruits which are unaccountably attractive to birds, and the Small guara (*G. coccinea,* p. 97), an inconspicuous weedy plant.

Bluebell, Harebell (*Campanula rotundifolia*). P. 98. The flowers are regular, with petals fused at the base to form the bell. The "Bluebell of Scotland" is a Campanula.

Blue aster (*Aster laevis*). P. 98. Blue to lavender composites. Most of the asters of the Mesa are white, the blue and lavender species being more abundant higher in the mountains. This species is still in flower in October. Asters have several rows of green scales under the ray flowers, the daisies (*Erigeron*) only a single

Wild geranium

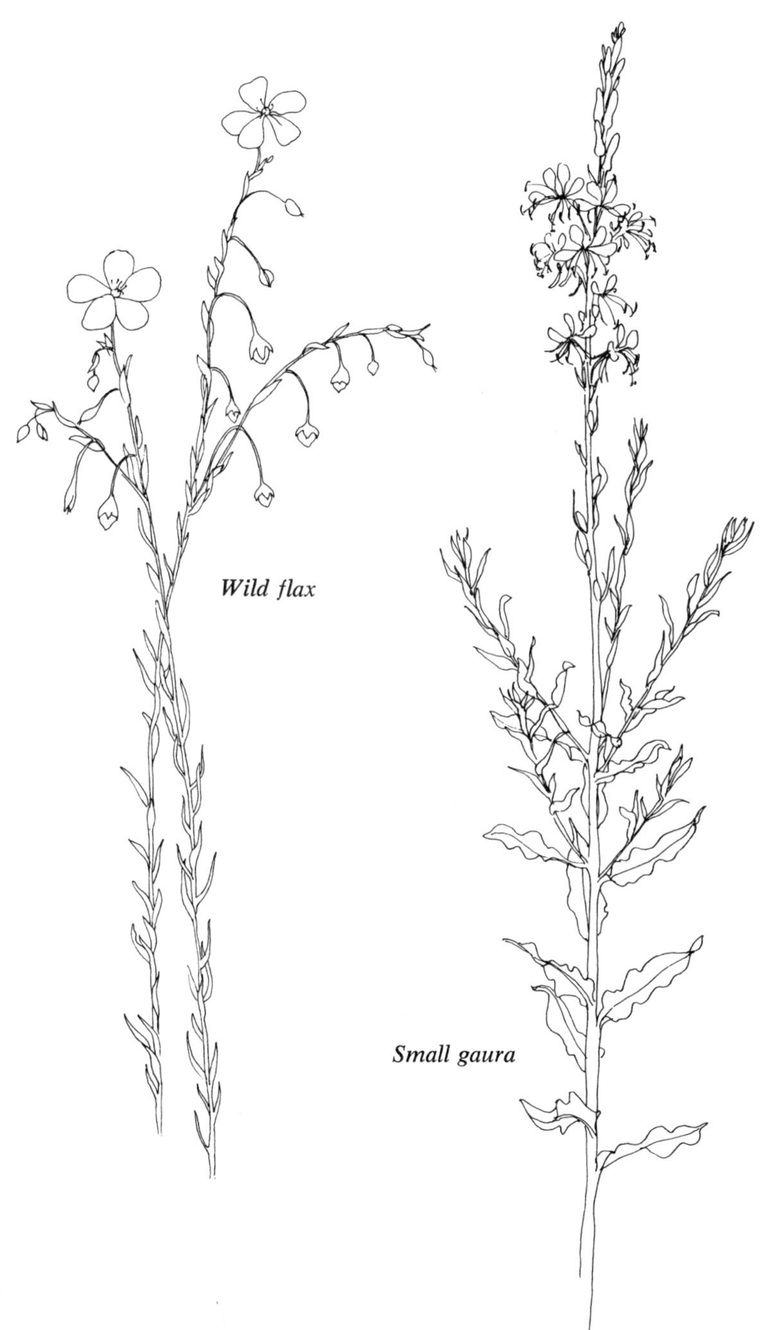

Wild flax
Small gaura

Blue aster
Bluebell

Immigrant thistle (*Carduus leiophyllus*). P. 101. About a dozen years ago this handsome thistle, with large bright purplish-red flower heads, was unknown in this part of Colorado; now it is the dominant thistle of the Mesa. Unlike the next species, which is comparable in appearance, the scales under the flower head are prickly.

Thistle (*Cirsium undulatum*). P. 100. The pale lavender flower heads are more delicate than those of the immigrant. The plant also is more likely to be found in the undisturbed natural vegetation of the mesa than the Immigrant thistle.

Canada thistle (*Cirsium arvense*). P. 101. Differs from the other thistles in having numerous small flower heads in clusters. They are various shades of purple, sometimes nearly white.

Chicory (*Cichorium undulatum*). P. 102. A flower of disturbed ground of the mesa roadsides. Survives for years in abandoned fields, where it makes an elegant spread of sky-blue flowers, or rather of flower heads, since it is a composite. White mutants are often seen. The heads close up by noon.

Blazing star (*Liatris punctata*). P. 102. This is a plant with many small composite flower heads in bloom simultaneously along much of the length of the single stalk, their powerful purple or magenta hue putting on a good show.

One-sided penstemon (*Penstemon secundifloris*). P. 103. A late spring and early summer species, with pink or pinkish-purple flowers, crowded to one side of the stalk. The large, clasping leaves look frost-covered.

Fat penstemon (*Penstemon virgatus*). P. 103. The irregular flower has the tubular base abruptly expanded into a healthy-looking large flower. Leaves green (not frosted), flowers blue.

Lupine (*Lupinus argenteus*). P. 104. In late summer this luxuriant blue-flowered bushy plant is a major contributor to the Mesa land-scape. Leaves are palmate, with more than five leaflets. The Texas blue-bonnet is closely related.

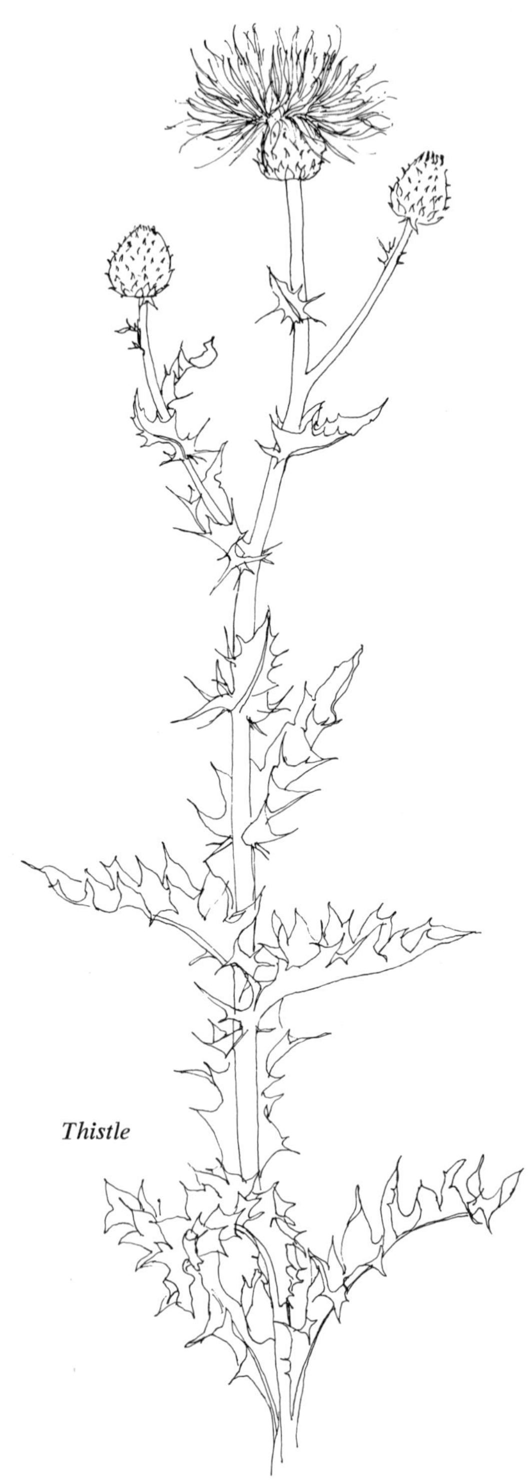

Thistle

Immigrant thistle
Canada thistle

Chicory
Blazing star

Fat penstemon

One-sided penstemon

Lupine

Scurf pea (*Psoralea tenuiflora* Pursh). P. 106. A legume with enamelled green leaflets that grows slowly but surely through the growing season to produce a crop of small inconspicuous purple flowers that appear even when the usual summer dry spell banishes most of the flowers. The scurf pea is then the mainstay of a variety of wild bees, all fast flyers that move quickly from one scanty flower to the next.

Purple prairie clover (*Dalea purpurea*). P. 106. The individual clover-like flowers are crowded onto a rather long single stalk, instead of the more globular head of the true clovers that grow in lawns. Flowers purplish-red with bright yellow stamens.

Purple peavine (*Lathyrus eucosmus*). P. 107. This tendril-bearing vine, a near relative of the garden sweet pea, sprawls out on the grassland, or can climb several feet up into bushes. Flowers purple or pink, irregular.

Bergamot, Pink bergamot (*Monarda fistulosa*). P. 108. Bergamot belongs to the mint family, which has square stems. The fragrant leaves are used to make bergamot tea. The pink to rose-purple irregular flowers, with long nectar-filled tubes, are much frequented by butterflies.

Coral-root orchid (*Corallorhiza wisteriana*). P. 108. Although only locally abundant, it is by far the most common orchid on the mesa, and in especially rainy years makes a respectable showing. Usually seen in the deep forest, where its pink stem, without a trace of green foliage, shows it to be a parasite. The irregular flowers vary from greenish yellow to purplish brown. Late spring and early summer.

Wild onion (*Allium*). Two of the species of wild onion found on the Mesa are generally pink or purplish-pink flowered. The Nodding onion (*A. cernuum*), p. 109, has a beautiful fireworks-shaped burst of lowers. The Three-leaved onion (*A. geyeri*), p. 109, has the flowers clustered in more prosaic fashion. Late spring.

Spiderwort (*Tradescantia occidentalis*). P. 110. The three large purple petals and broad grass-like leaves are distinctive.

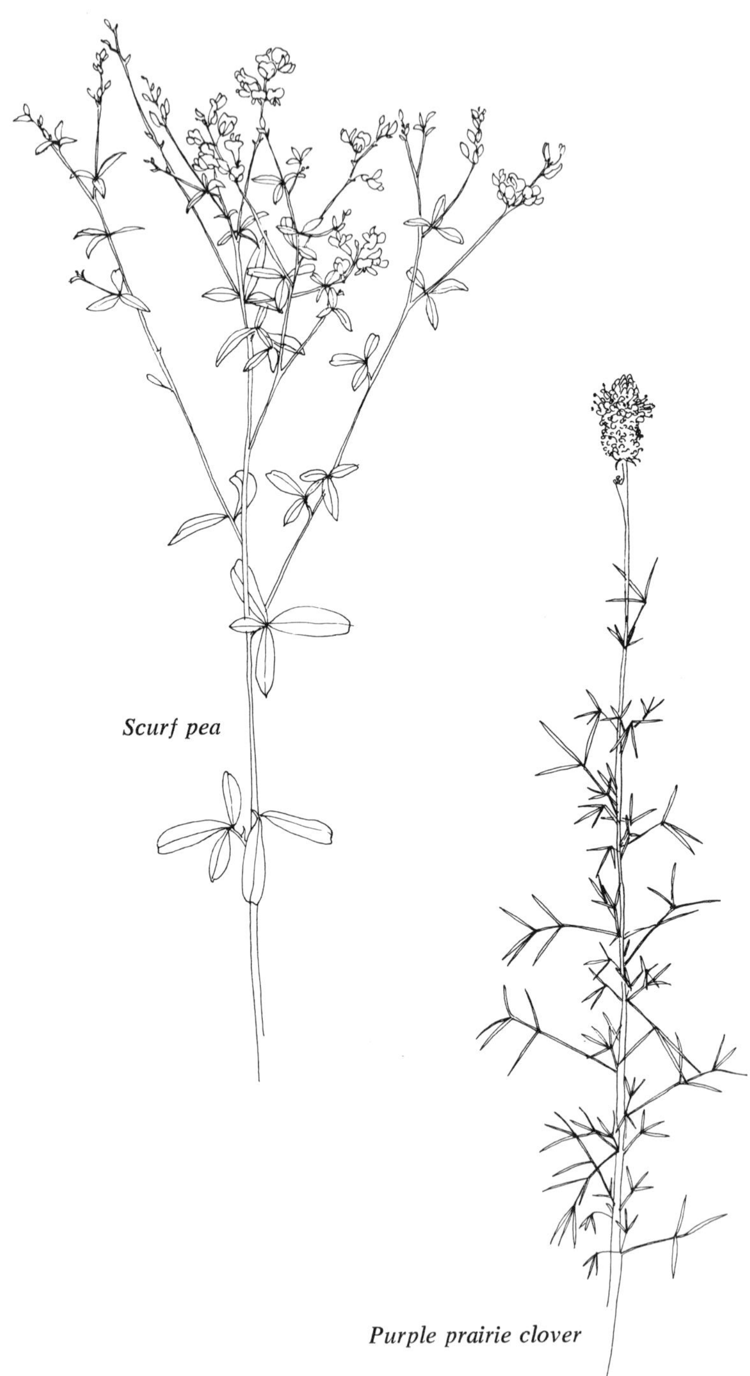

Scurf pea

Purple prairie clover

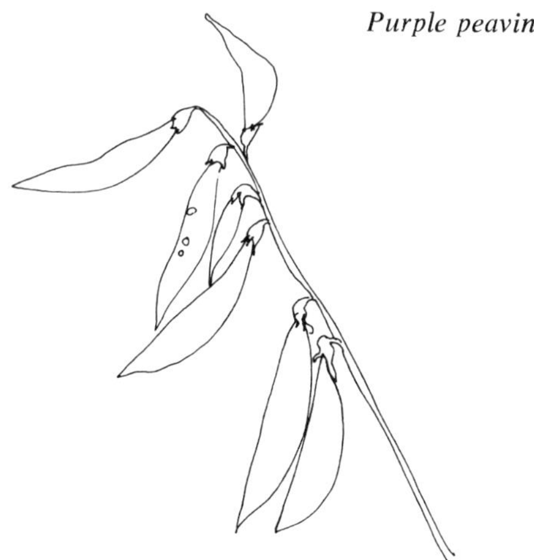

Purple peavine

Pink bergamot

Coral-root orchid

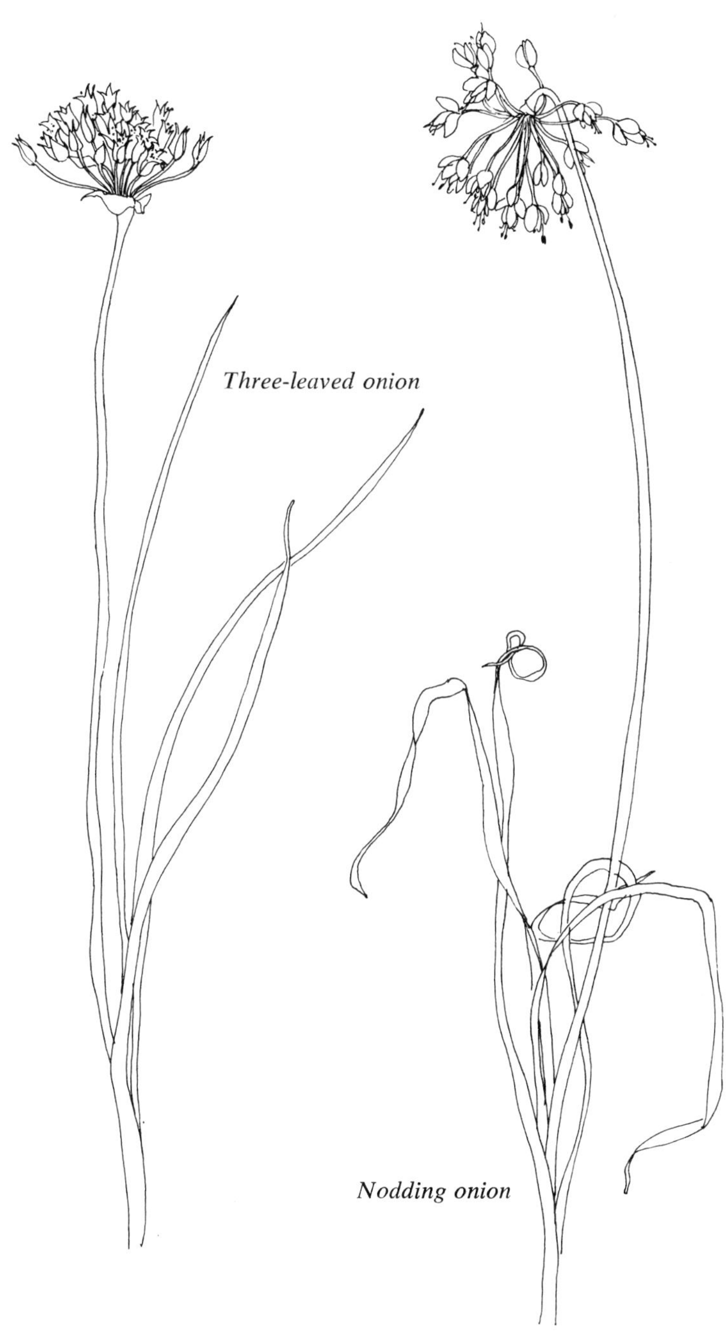

Three-leaved onion
Nodding onion

Spiderwort

Wild iris
Blue gentian

Blue flag, Wild iris (*Iris missouriensis*). P. 111. These spectacular flowers bloom in late spring and early summer. A large field of them can be seen in the valley above and to the south of the sweeping curve on the road up NCAR mesa.

Blue gentian (*Gentiana affinis*). P. 111. By early fall, this is almost the only non-composite flower left blooming on the mesa. After a fall rain, the clean, blue flowers of this gentian come as a pleasant surprise in the drab grasslands.

FLOWERS WHITE, OFF-WHITE

Sandwort (*Arenaria fendleri*). P. 113. These small, white-flowered plants with grass-like leaves follow their near relative, the Mouse-ear, in the late spring as one of the common mesa flowers.

Thimbleweed (*Anemone cylindrica*). P. 113. The regular, open flowers have greenish-white "petals" (actually sepals converted into petal-like structures). In the center of the flowers, the ovaries grow into an aggregation of fruits heaped up like a slender thimble.

Prickly poppy (*Argemone*). P. 114. The large white, floppy flowers are unmistakable. Perhaps two similar species on the mesa. The plant is as prickly as a thistle.

Bedstraw (*Galium boreale*). P. 115. The small white flowers are clustered. Leaves in whorls of four. A related species is fragrant when dried, and it has been used for mattresses, hence the name.

Goosegrass (*Galium aparine*). P. 114. A weak, sticky-clinging sprawling relative of the Bedstraw, with numerous leaves in each whorl. Shown here in fruit.

Bouncing Bet, Soapwort (*Saponaria officinalis*). P. 115. Especially abundant along roadsides. A long-established escape from gardens. The leaves can be lathered up in water. Flowers white to pale pink.

Sandwort

Thimbleweed

113

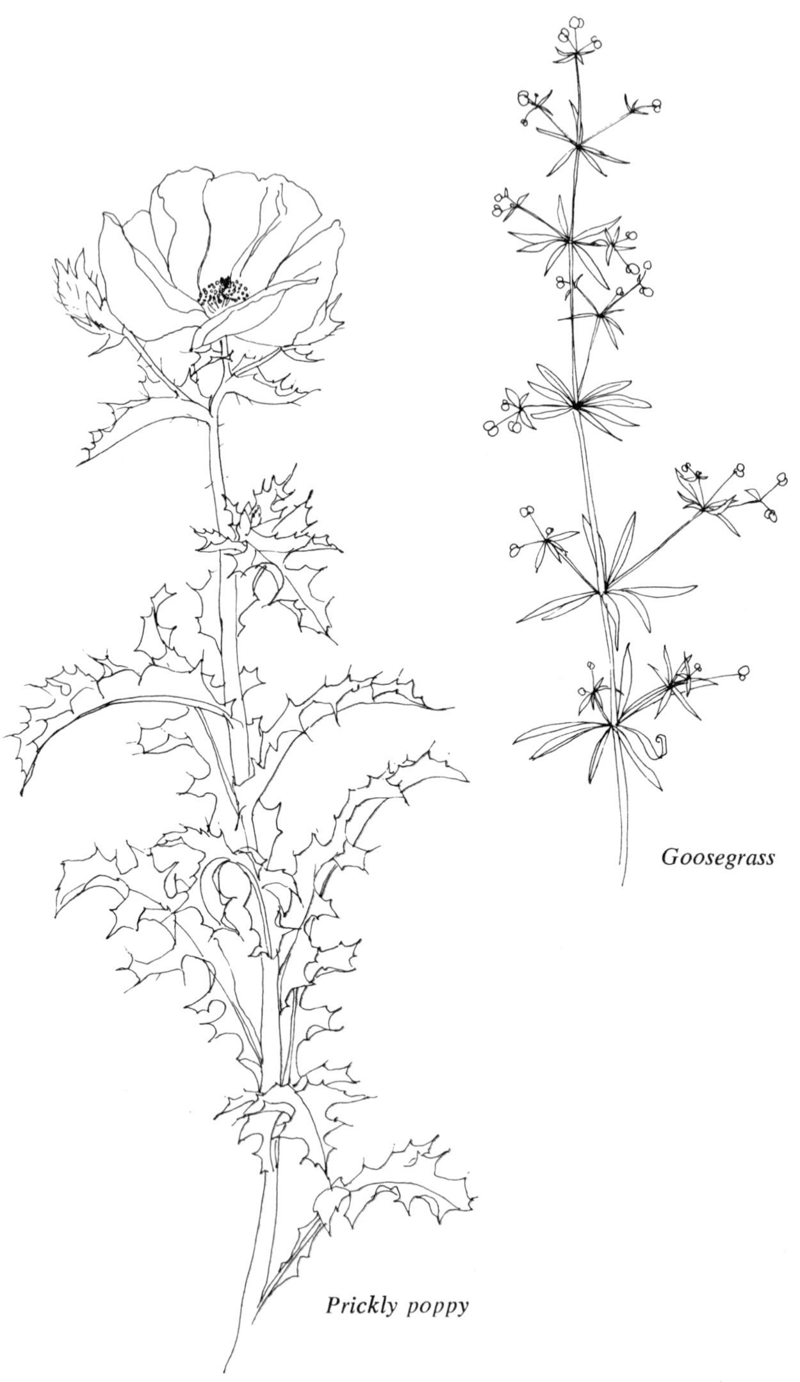

Goosegrass

Prickly poppy

114

Bedstraw

Bouncing Bet

Bushy sulfur plant
Bastard toad flax

Bushy sulfur plant (*Eriogonum effusum*). P. 116. The small flowers, white to pinkish, are abundant on these low, bushy plants. They look much the same alive or dead, so are sometimes picked when in flower for future use in winter flower arrangements.

Bastard toad flax (*Comandra umbellata*). P. 116. A small plant with small white flowers. Rather characterless; said to be partially parasitic on other flowers.

Monument plant. Green gentian (*Frasera speciosa*). P. 118. With huge basal leaves. Bears a massive flower stalk with good-sized, beautifully sculptured, greenish-white flowers.

Scorpion weed (*Phacelia heterophylla*). P. 119. The flower buds are in a tight coil, which partially straightens out as the white flowers open. A coarse, bristly-hairy plant. Late spring and early summer.

Miner's candle (*Cryptantha virgata*). P. 120. A rough-hairy plant, prickly to the touch. Pollen sacs are well down into the tube of the white flowers, and several groups of bees have become adapted to gathering the pollen by evolving recurved hooks on their tongues.

False boneset (*Kuhnia eupatorioides*). P. 120. The narrow composite flower heads are not showy, and are off-white in color.

Low daisy (*Erigeron pumilus*). P. 121. Unopened flower head is rosy-pink, but as rays open out, the "petals" appear white. Late spring and summer.

White aster (*Aster*). There are two abundant species of white aster on the mesa in the late summer and early fall: *A. porteri* (p. 122), with more slender leaves and the flower heads more widely scattered on the plant, and *A. falcatus* (p. 122), with wider leaves and the flower heads bunched closely together.

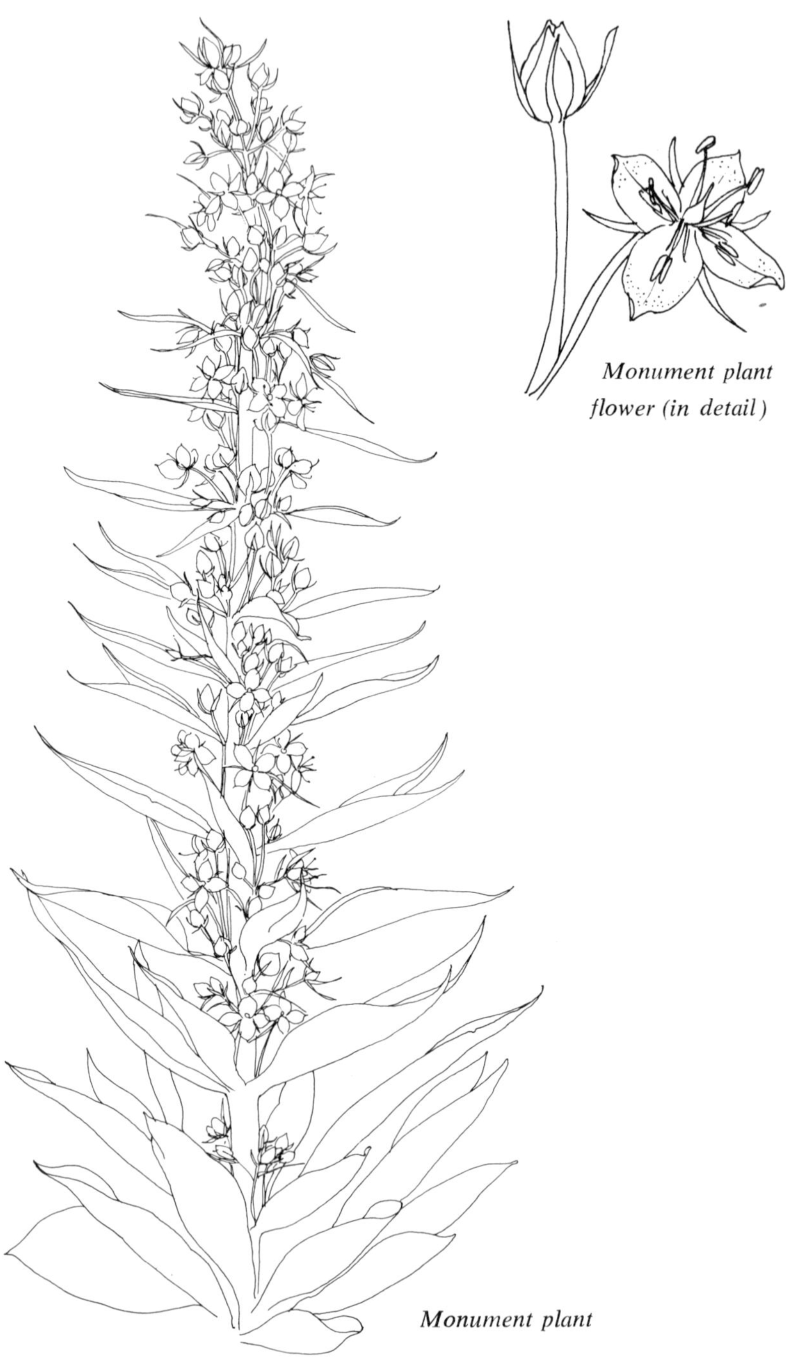

*Monument plant
flower (in detail)*

Monument plant

Scorpion weed

False boneset

Miners candle

Yarrow
Low daisy

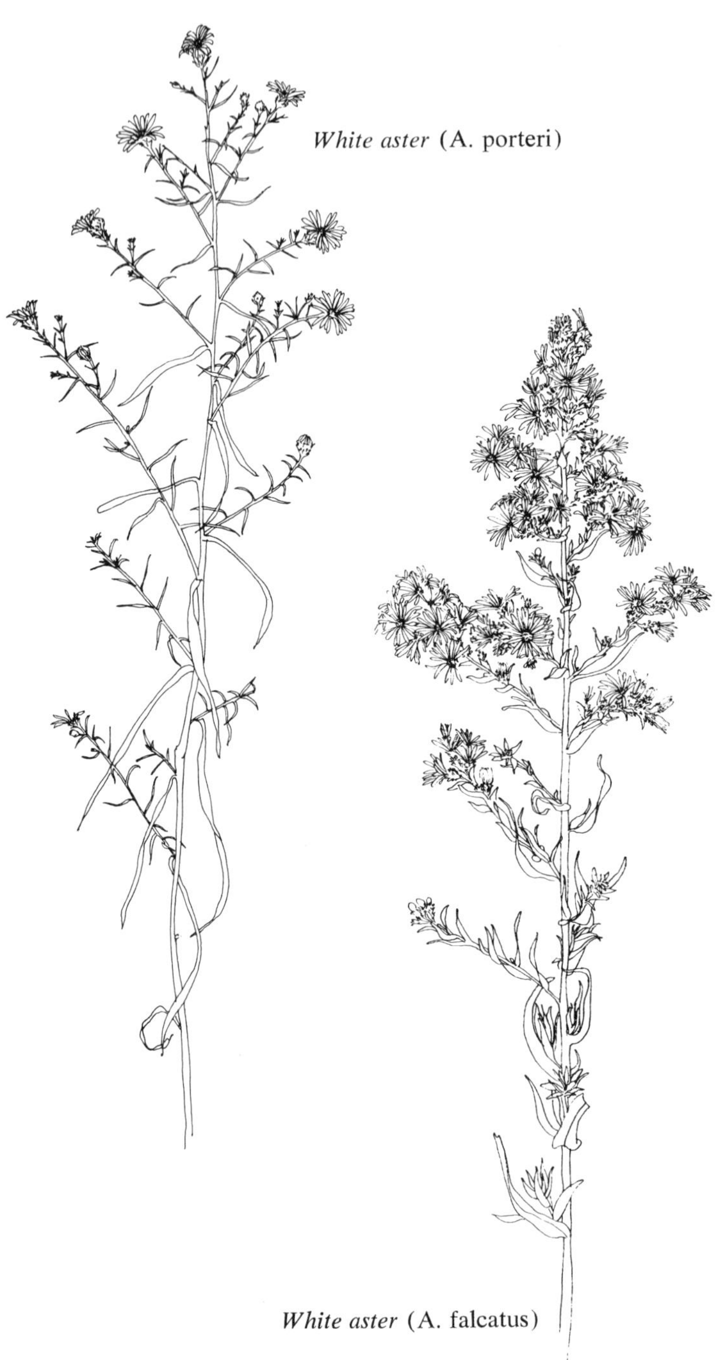

White aster (A. porteri)

White aster (A. falcatus)

Large Easter daisy

Yarrow (*Achillea lanulosa*). P. 121. A dull white-flowered composite, but the individual heads are very small, and clustered into tight groupings, like an umbellifer. The fern-like leaves are aromatic.

Large Easter daisy (*Townsendia grandiflora*). P. 123. A large version of the early spring *T. hookeri,* but with long stems. Rays white.

Licorice root (*Glycyrrhiza lepidota*). P. 124. A tall, weedy legume with inconspicuous small white flowers, usually at lower entrances of mesa canyons. Does not attract attention until it comes into fruit. The only legume hereabouts with "cockleburs".

White peavine (*Lathyrus leucanthus*). P. 124. A low sweetpea-like vine with white flowers; on mesa slopes, often in colonies.

White prairie clover (*Dalea candida*). P. 125. A white-flowered counterpart of the purple prairie clover; see this in preceding section.

Licorice root (in fruit)

White peavine

White prairie clover

Snow-on-the-mountain (*Euphorbia marginata*). P. 127. Although the true flowers of this plant are inconspicuous, the plant is showy because the uppermost leaves have white margins, using the same strategy for attracting pollinators as the closely related Christmas poinsettia. The plant is protected by a poisonous milky sap.

Narrow-leaved milkweed (*Asclepias stenophyllus*). P. 128. This narrow-leaved plant, with a slender pod and less than knee-high, bears little resemblance to the gigantic milkweeds, with large pods, that are common on the nearby irrigated plains. The flowers are white.

Low milkweed (*Asclepias pumila*). P. 129. Even smaller than the Narrow-leaved milkweed. Like all *Asclepias*, it has milky sap.

Arrowhead (*Sagittaria*). P. 129. Grows in the shallow edges of the mesa ponds. There are two closely related species.

Yucca, Spanish bayonet (*Yucca glauca*). P. 131. A most familiar part of the mesa scenery, with its cluster of stiff, sharp, grass-like leaves. Is functionally, but not botanically, often considered a cactus. The white flowers have the structure of lilies, the family to which it belongs.

Mariposa lily (*Calochortus gunnisonii*). P. 130. On favorable years there may be hundreds of these elegant, white flowered lilies in view at one time on the mesa hillsides.

Two-leaved onion (*Allium textile*). P. 130. This is yet another lily of the mesa grasslands.

Poison hemlock (*Conium maculatum*). A huge weed, more than head high, with large umbels of small white flowers, fern-like leaves, and purplish spots on the thick, hollow stems. There is a forest of these in the lower reaches of Skunk Canyon. Not shown here.

126

Snow-on-the-mountain

Narrow-leaved milkweed

ERRATA

P. 14, line 11: *Spiraea*

P. 30, lines 11-30: *Artemisia*

P. 33, line 7: *Echinocereus viridiflorus*

P. 38, line 3: "p. 64" should read "p. 63".

P. 38, line 4: "P. 42" should read "P. 40".

P. 38, line 8: *Musineon divaricatum*

P. 48, line 8: "back" should read "black"

P. 50, line 3: "The same" should read "A related".

P. 62, line 1: *Viola pedatifida*

P. 67, line 22: Death camas
Zygadenus venenosus

P. 71: Death camas

P. 79, line 1: *Oenothera brachycarpa*

P. 95, line 1: *Castilleja miniata*

P. 95, end of bottom line: Add "row".

P. 99, line 14: *Cichorium intybus*

P. 138, lines 23, 25: Steller's jay

Arrowhead
Low milkweed

Mariposa lily
Two-leaved onion

Yucca

INSECTS

There probably are two or three thousand species of insects that regularly occur in the grasslands, forests, thickets, and ponds of the Enchanted Mesa, so that the account that follows is necessarily only fragmentary. Some of these species are represented by millions of individuals, and are important in the food economy of the mesa, both as eaters and the eaten. Their bodies are rich in protein and fat, and are the main diet for the ravenous broods of song birds that are raised on the mesa each year.

The most worrisome and unaesthetic of the "insects" to the experienced hiker of the mesas and foothills is the woodtick, which is not an insect at all, but an 8-legged distant relative of the insects. Woodticks appear on the mesa as early as March and flourish in April and on into early May, their abundance varying a good deal with the weather. These flattened, shiny brown creatures fasten on to the skin by their beaks to suck blood, and are loaded with organisms of disease. Two of the most feared diseases are Colorado tick fever, caused by a virus which is common in ticks of the Boulder area, and Rocky Mountain spotted fever, caused by a rickettsia, and relatively uncommon here. The first is unpleasant, non-fatal, and unaffected by antibiotics; the second is also unpleasant, but often fatal if not treated soon enough with antibiotics. Anyone who spends much time in the field would do well to read up on the woodtick in a modern textbook on medical entomology. The casual hiker should take the trouble to see to it that no woodtick spends any considerable time with its beak embedded in his skin, since the chance of infection increases rapidly with duration of attachment. This takes constant vigilance in the foothills and mesa country at the height of the tick season. The bite is usually completely painless when inflicted, although it may produce a welt that itches for weeks afterward.

There are few confirmed biters among the true insects of the mesa. Mosquitos are usually uncommon. The only really competent molesters are the species of deerfly of high summer, with large, beautifully banded iridescent eyes, and an oath-wringing bite. Ants generally find you if you spend any length of time on dry sandy ground. Fortunately, our species usually nip (and that rather reluctantly) rather than sting, with consequences of non-medical significance.

Two groups of insects are abundant, large, active, and colorful enough that they form a conspicuous part of the landscape: the butterflies, and some of the grasshoppers. There are perhaps no more than a half dozen species or species groups of butterflies that are common and large enough to qualify as ordinary scenery, although the dedicated butterfly collector, with trained eye and a knowledge of where colonies exist in just the right ecological situations, can ferret out ten times this number. Fortunately, for the serious student there is a book, *Colorado Butterflies* by Brown, Eff, and Rotger. Don Eff is a Boulder resident, so our butterflies are well known.

First of the abundant butterflies, appearing in late April and early May are the Marbles, with the engaging technical name of *Euchloe*. These span a little more than an inch, are white above, and yellowish green below. The under side of the hindwing has a coarse network of silvery green markings, which gives these butterflies their common name. There are two species, one distinguished by a delicate rose flush on the wings, which can be seen only at close range.

Also early in the spring, one encounters at the banks of rain pools bits of the clearest Colorado sky flitting about, taking drinks from the moist sand. These are the Spring azures, or blues, members of a group of butterflies with a dozen or more species in the area, many of them bronze, and a couple of them with shining green undersides to the wings.

Towards the end of May there appears the commonest butterfly of the Mesa, the Ochre ringlet, *Coenonympha tullia*. This small butterfly, spanning less than an inch, is a plain orange-brown above, and marked below with a few small eye-like patterns whose beauty can only be appreciated under a lens. The caterpillars are grass-eaters, and these rather sedentary butterflies are found mainly in the grassy meadows.

Somewhat later, the flashy tribe of fritillaries (species of the genus *Speyeria*), which may span nearly 3 inches, make their appearance, and persist until the end of the growing season. Most of these tawny-brown species have, on the underside of the wings, large silver spots that look as if made of beaten silver. The butterfly specialists wrangle interminably over the "right name" for individuals of this bewilderingly diverse group. The earliest and commonest is a showy and distinct species, *Speyeria edwardsi,* named after one of the pioneer students of western American butterflies, W. H. Edwards.

By mid-July, a large relative of the Ochre ringlet, called the Eyed woodnymph, becomes abundant. This dark brown butterfly has eye-spots on the underside that are blue-centered in the female. These, like the ringlet, have grass-eating caterpillars, and the butterflies are most common, especially after the females have appeared in early August, in the lush vegetation of the canyons, in such localities as the mouth of Fern Canyon or of Shadow Canyon.

Toward the end of July the pine forests are brought to life by the Pine white, a strong-flying butterfly that spans two inches, with the wings decorated with black markings, and some added splashes of red in the female. These lay their eggs on the needles of the Ponderosa pine, and usually are seen flying well up in the trees. During July they reach a peak of abundance on the lower slopes of the adjacent foothills, then abruptly disappear near the end of August.

The grasshoppers that live in the garden and the lush weeds of vacant lots are for the most part a sluggish and unpleasant lot, distinguished mainly by their voracity, but among the wild species of the mesa are some splendidly dashing and butterfly-colored specimens, wary of the intruder and able to escape with swift and controlled flight. In earliest spring are some that fly up to reveal scarlet hind wings. When they alight, these wide hind wings fold up like a fan to be concealed by the narrow front wings which are exactly the color of the place where the grasshopper lands. Some individuals of this species have yellow hind wings, others orange. It is believed that there is a simple genetic basis to this variety of color, and the orange-winged individuals are hybrids between the red and yellow. During the hot days of August, the Carolina locust (*Dissosteir*a) gives life to the dusty roads, rising up in a dancing flight on wide black wings that are edged with yellow.

If one stands quietly in a flowery meadow on a still summer day, one hears a powerful, all-pervasive hum, the sound of the wings of thousands of mostly unseen insects, pursuing their manifold pleasures in the sky and in the labyrinths of the vegetation cover. Nearly all of this flight is powered by the nectar of flowers. A great variety of insects, chiefly two-winged flies (*Diptera*) and the bees and wasps (*Hymenoptera*), are nectar drinkers, but the bees are the insects most uniformly and best adapted to feed on flowers, using both nectar and pollen, and rearing their young on this rich and delicious mixture, which is obtained only by the intelligent expenditure of a good deal of energy by the female parent.

The famous pioneer authority on wild bees, T. D. A. Cockerell, was for many years a professor of biology at the University of Colorado. Being the first student of bees in the Rocky Mountain West, he found on the mesas and in the higher ranges many species hitherto unknown to science. Boulder is therefore the "type" locality for many species of bees. The casual observer of the flower-visiting bees on the mesa (many of the wild bees look quite different from the domestic honeybee) will note that there are some that carry the pollen (which is to be transported back to the nest to make a food store for the young) in large masses on the hind legs, and another group of bees that carries it in a brush on the underside of the body.

By midsummer the most powerful and predatory of the two-winged flies have become common enough to attract notice. These are the robber-flies, the largest of which have slender bodies an inch and a half long. They perch on outlooks a foot or so above the ground, then launch themselves with almost invisible speed after other insects that happen by, which they snatch out of the air. Taking the victim to a resting place, they insert their sharp, drinking-straw beak, quickly kill the prey with venom, turn the inside to a liquid with copious digestive juices poured into it, and drink the nutritious beverage. Often the first indication one has of the presence of the robber flies is the abrupt, short burst of the high whine made by their powerful wings.

On the mesas between Bear Canyon and South Boulder Creek are 5 small ponds, the largest sometimes with a sheet of water 50 feet or more across, which were constructed when the area was ranchland. Now that cattle have been almost completely excluded from the mesa land, these ponds are usually permanent, and in them lives a rich variety of animals and plants. Most of these are microscopic, but among the animals are several species of good-sized insects, including waterboatmen, backswimmers, and several kinds of beetles. These are air breathers, and are usually seen when they come to the surface to capture an air bubble, which they carry around with them under water until it wears out and they have to come up for another. Also in the pond are the young of the dragonflies and damsel flies, which can be seen by dredging up the muck from the bottom of the pond. However, the fully-grown insect is a splendid winged creature of the skies, and the several species of large mature dragon flies, with wing spans of a few inches, are among the conspicuous insects of the mesa, which they patrol in search of the flying insects that are their prey.

Toward the end of June, one hears up in the pines a stealthy soft clicking sound. This is the song of a tiny cicada, *Platypedia putnami*. Its large relatives out on the plains make a piercing ringing noise like that of a large buzzsaw.

In September, the air is filled with the songs of insects, although for the most part there are only two performers in the orchestra: the husky black field cricket (*Gryllus*), which plays a succession of loud, piercing chirps, and the tree cricket (*Oecanthus*), a delicate, very pale insect that is usually up off the ground, clinging to vegetation, which tirelessly sings a long, steady, musical trill. The singers are all males, and the instruments are the resonant front wings, which have a washboard-like surface at the base of one wing and a scraper on the other.

AMPHIBIANS

As soon as the ice melts off the mesa ponds and the pools of the small streams in the canyons, the winter silence is broken by another chorus of trills and chirps. Although there is a spring generation of field crickets, most of the early spring music is that of two kinds of frogs, the tiny tree frogs, *Pseudacris* (which in Colorado do not live in trees), and the medium-sized Leopard frog (*Rana pipiens*), green with black spots. Toads are present, but are rarely seen or heard. At least two of the ponds swarm with salamanders or "water dogs" (*Ambystoma tigrinum*). These water-dwelling salamanders look like fish with legs, but have entirely different gills, which sprout externally from the back of the head. At low altitude these salamanders lose their gills and climb out onto the land to spend some time roaming about, but at higher altitudes they stay in the water. Although they keep their juvenile appearance, they reproduce anyway. Such gilled forms are known as axolotls, the Central American sound of the name being due to the fact of their original discovery in the high lakes of Mexico.

REPTILES

Snakes and lizards make themselves very inconspicuous on the mesa. During the hundreds of hours I have spent walking the mesas I have never seen a rattlesnake. It may be that they no longer inhabit the area, since they are said to retreat quickly before human disturbance. I have seen several in the lower foothills between Left Hand Canyon and the Little Thompson Canyon, some miles north of Boulder. The snakes (all nonvenomous) that one most often blunders into on the mesa are the Green racer (*Coluber*), which is without a color pattern, the Bull snake (*Pituophis*), of pleasing orange brown color with darker blotches on the back, and the striped garter snake (*Thamnophis*), usually seen near the streamlets. The Bull snake has a color pattern something like that of a rattler, and sometimes vibrates the tip of the tail in dry grass to make a buzzing sound. Even the commonest lizard of the Mesa (*Sceloporus*), a small lizard seen running about on the rocks, is not often encountered. It is nearly impossible to find, on order, one of the Horned lizards or Horned "toads", which occur sparingly in the region.

BIRDS

On a certain 12th of May, my field notes on Shanahan Mesa maintain that the air was filled with the "caroling of robins, the mourning of doves, and the pealing of meadowlarks." Although on some days, even in summer, one may walk for an hour through silent woods, without seeing a bird, it is these animals, close relatives of the reptiles, but hot-blooded animals with a brain kept sharp by a constant operating temperature, that dominate the larger animate life of the mesa during the day.

Here, as in the descriptions of other groups of organisms, for the most part only those species likely to come to the attention of the casual observer are mentioned. The dedicated bird watcher will find the mesa land an inexhaustible field of study, and will find several specialized books and papers to guide him.

The bird that surprises the Easterner is the beautiful magpie, with its bold black and white markings and long, streaming tail. It lives on the mesa the year round. Its spherical nests, about the size of a bushel basket and made of coarse twigs, are common in the pines and the deciduous trees of the canyons. The nest is begun in the cold raw weather of March; there are eggs by mid-April; and by mid-June the young—sometimes six or eight in a brood—are flying, even though they are still bob-tailed.

Another common and conspicuous year-round resident of the mesa land is the Stellar's jay, a near relative of the eastern Blue jay, but with more sophisticated, subdued coloring, a soft shading of deep blue and purple. Like the Magpie, the Stellar's jay indulges in long soliloquies, complicated mixtures of grating and whistling noises intermingled with brief musical passages.

The newcomer from the East will also be surprised by the call of the Western meadowlark, which has a bold, triumphant quality lacking in the eastern species. Occasionally the bird, while in flight, goes wild with a cascade of hundreds of notes that carry only traces of melody. The meadowlark is common on the mesa, and nests in the grassland.

By far the most brilliant of the commoner birds of the mesa is the Western tanager. It is a robin-sized bird, and the male has a red head, a bright yellow body, and black wings. One would think that they would make the pines look like Christmas trees, but in fact these birds manage to make themselves rather unobtrusive. They are more common than one might think; a careful observer noted four active nests in an area of about as many acres.

One of the commoner of the "little gray birds" (LGBs), judging from the frequency of its loud, cheerful song is the Solitary vireo. Sometimes when one follows up the song, he finds that he has been led to the nest, an elegant little cup built in the lower branches of a pine tree. The mate, sitting on the nest, merely looks at the intruder in trusting fashion, and will even allow a person to stroke its back without leaving the nest.

Another of the common LGBs is a small flycatcher (*Empidonax*), which sits upright on a good vantage point, occasionally emitting a dry, insect-like trill, and launching forth now and then to catch a flying insect with a loud, popping snap of the bill.

Commonest of the summer sparrows is the diminutive chipping sparrow, with a bright red-brown cap, and a habit of singing sleepily well into the dusk.

The mourning dove is heard more often than seen. It often makes its nest, a slight platform of twigs, on the open ground, even though the eggs are shining white, without the protective coloration of the eggs of most ground-nesting birds, and even though trees are close by. Some do nest in the pine trees, the nests so flimsy that the eggs can sometimes be seen from below. The bird has a very small head.

A paradise for birds is afforded by the thickets at the bottom of the canyons. The most outstanding citizen here is the Spotted towhee, which sits boldly on the highest perch to sing his simple song. Among other residents are the House Wren (which in the West avoids houses), Chat, Catbird, and Lazuli bunting. Probably over the years one could observe well over a hundred species of birds on the mesa, either as residents or as transients.

A bird rather rare on the mesa (but which makes itself widely known) is the poor-will, which calls its name in the late evening. Its near relative, the nighthawk, flies high in the sky, calling a coarse "jeep, jeep" as it flies a zig-zag pattern on its long, narrow wings in pursuit of insects. Occasionally, perhaps to impress a lady acquaintance, it makes a long dive, and in the pull-out the wing or tail feathers are vibrated to produce a loud musical twang.

A pair of eagles still nests somewhere in the crags of Bear Canyon, since a pair of young are seen in the area in mid-summer nearly every year, along with the parents. I have seen an adult laboring in heavy flight up the canyon with a full-grown jackrabbit dangling from its claws. The birds and mammals of the mesa live constantly under the threat of a few hawks and falcons—the Prairie falcon, Sparrow hawk (another falcon), Sharp-shin hawk, Cooper's hawk, and a Goshawk. Both the Cooper's and the Sharp-shin—hawks with short wings that like to fly low at break-neck speed through the forest and shrubbery—make a habit of patrolling the bird-feeding stations in the suburbs just below the NCAR mesa, hurtling through the yards between houses and instantly freezing the small songbirds into silent immobility.

MAMMALS

A hundred years ago elk, grizzly bears, buffalo, antelope, and mule deer flourished in the rich lands at the intersection of the plains and mountains in the Boulder area; of these, only the deer remains today. It is common on the mesas, and Boulder residents often drive up the NCAR road at dusk to see the deer grazing peacefully in the meadows. The hiker, as often as not, disturbs a resting herd when he cuts cross-country in the daytime through the forest.

The only other mammal, besides human beings and their dogs, that is large enough to be seen with any regularity on the mesa is the beautiful tuft-eared squirrel, with a body a foot long, a bushy tail, and luxuriously hairy ears. It is "supposed" to be light gray above, white beneath, but in the Boulder region many or most are genetic mutants that are coal black or dark brown in color. Whether or not this is a situation that has developed near civilization, where the number of predators that would normally kill off squirrels not protectively colored is lessened, is not known.

Cottontail rabbits are sometimes seen. In mid-July, the young are about, some so small and trusting that it seems impossible that they could take care of themselves; no doubt many of them do not. Jack-rabbits, both white-tailed and black, seem to have become even more scarce in the past few years.

Porcupines are known to be present on the mesa mainly by the results of their feeding on the inner bark of the upper trunk and branches of the pine trees. Usually they do not completely girdle the trunk. Once I watched, from a distance of three feet, a porcupine eating the flowers of thornapple, delicately gathering them in with his paws. Another time I found in the forest a flattened-out skin of a freshly killed porcupine, indicating that there may still be a predator in the area capable of dealing with this formidably defended animal; bobcats and mountain lions are known to be able to do so.

Red foxes are seen occasionally, coyotes rarely.

Marmots or woodchucks, heavily-bodied, good-sized rodents that live close to a shelter under a rock, and often stand up straight and whistle loudly, are found here and there over the mesa lands. The stone fence and large boulders near the Dunn House, at the south end of the Mesa trail, is a favorite resort for these animals. For a couple of seasons there was a large marmot that climbed the highest boulder along the trail to "greet" (maybe it was to complain about) each hiker that came along. For a few days one spring I failed to see it, and looking among the rocks I found blue plastic casings of shotgun shells. The many hikers that use this part of the trail now miss the cheerful whistle of this marmot.

Most abundant of the mammals on the mesa is the Deer mouse (*Peromyscus*), which is mainly nocturnal, so not usually seen. These are attractive creatures, tawny brown above and pure white below, with large ears and with a long tail that gives them good balance while climbing in the shrubbery. They feed not only on vegetation but also on insects and may in part at least account for the shyness of crickets and katydids that sing in the night, but abruptly become silent as one approaches.